Police Perspective:

Life on the Beat

25th Anniversary Edition

Gail
I hope you
enjoy the book.
Best Wishes)

John Matthews

This book is dedicated to
Jill, David, Mark, Megan,
Michael, Joseph and Isabella

"Remembrance of things past are not always remembrances of things as they were."

-Marcel Proust

Foreword

Twenty-five years ago, destiny—or fate, depending on one's perspective—brought together Joe Whitney, owner and editor of the *Oak Cliff Tribune,* and me, a Dallas Police Officer. At the time I was assigned to the newly-created Jefferson Boulevard police storefront, and Joe was an integral part of the revitalization efforts taking place in Oak Cliff. Never having been accused of being a wallflower, I promptly approached Joe with the idea of my writing an occasional article for his paper. Being a visionary and an out-of-the-box-thinking businessman, Joe agreed to give it a try, and we discussed what the proposed article might be called. I didn't necessarily have a name in mind, but (always fond of alliteration) told him I would simply give him my "police perspective." With that, a new column was born.

Little did either of us imagine then that the "occasional article" would quickly evolve into a popular weekly feature in the *Tribune.* Within the blink of an eye came a Texas Press Association award for column writing. I thought that was the highlight of my career—until I received a call from two-time Edgar Award-winning author Carlton Stowers, who said he was a fan of the column and who encouraged me to write a book based on my investigation and arrest of Dallas's only serial killer. It seemed that I had barely recovered from that amazing phone call before Pinnacle Books was publishing The Eyeball Killer, co-written with journalist Christine Wicker. It was my first mass market book and led to a string of popular television shows "based on fact," and documentaries which would retell the story in various formats for the next two decades.

The success of the first book solidified my desire to keep writing long after *Police Perspective* and the *Oak Cliff Tribune* faded from sight. Over the years I have written and published numerous articles for a variety of magazines, scores of national public safety training programs and trade publications, a book series on school safety resulting in the 2004 USA Best Book Finalist *School Safety 101*, and *Mass Shootings: Six Steps to Survival*, which I frequently refer to in my appearances on CNN and FOX News as a law enforcement analyst and policing expert.

Now, some 25 years after that first fateful meeting with Joe, we've come full circle. This book is not just a compilation of old tales but also presents articles that were never published, as well as a sampling of never-before-seen stories. Some stories because of their length never made it past the cutting room floor, while others I simply kept to myself for reasons even a writer has difficulty explaining.

Over the years, people have asked me if all the stories I told were true. I always told them that—like many a television writer before me—my stories are always "based on fact," however you want to interpret that: as sloppy note-taking, creative writing, or just faded memories of days gone by.

This is my Bella book, affectionately named for my youngest child, Isabella Grace Matthews. The many trips to my wife's doctor in Oak Cliff evoked powerful memories of driving those streets, and became the genesis of this book. So, in celebration of the 25th anniversary of my column, here is my potpourri of police perspectives.

Introduction

After more than three decades spent behind the badge, it is time to reflect on some of my stories from walking the beat in Oak Cliff. Tales that have shaped my memories, dreams—even nightmares—call after call, night after night. My eight-hour home was a section of Dallas that has often been referred to as "The Hidden City." Many Oak Cliff residents agree that the general boundaries are Interstate 35 (some say Beckley Avenue) on the east, Camp Wisdom on the south, Loop 12 to the west, and Interstate 30 or the Trinity River to the north. To others—especially in the media—for too long, Oak Cliff was "wherever the latest crime spree was occurring."

This section of the city with its population of several hundred thousand is as diverse as anywhere in the nation, with White, Black, and Hispanic living alongside a host of other ethnic groups and nationalities, its residents ranging from rich to middle class to extremely poor. Officers working in North Oak Cliff can respond to a call for service in a million-dollar mansion in Kessler Park one minute and turn right around and respond to tenants of Section 8 housing the next.

It is not my intention to paint a negative picture of Oak Cliff or the city of Dallas, although at times it seemed as though I had been thrust into middle of Dante's Inferno, as I encountered gang shooting after sexual assault after murder.

As fate would have it, my years in "The Cliff" were some of the most violent in the history of Dallas, with annual homicides surpassing 500 for the first time ever, and gang violence ripping the city apart. For years the "official line" of the city was that Dallas simply did not have gangs as did New York, Chicago, or Los Angeles. But with the body counts rising with each passing day, the city was finally forced to admit that we had a gang problem. When the official policy changed almost overnight, we went from "no recognized gangs" to nearly two hundred formal gangs with over six thousand members. I guess that was one of our bad nights.

For years, local historians and private companies have hosted crime tours of Oak Cliff's most notorious sites. They visit the grave of the infamous Clyde Barrow, the West Dallas thug who made criminal history with his partner Bonnie Parker; the El Dorado Street house of Charles Albright, better known as Dallas's Eyeball Killer; and the famous landmarks from the Kennedy assassination including the house where Lee Harvey Oswald lived, the Texas Theater on Jefferson Blvd where Oswald was captured, the apartment where Oswald's killer Jack Ruby once lived, and the intersection of Patton and Tenth where Dallas Officer J.D. Tippit was allegedly murdered by Oswald.

As the residents of Oak Cliff are eager to point out, there are many beautiful places in this community. As a matter of fact, some of my proudest moments as an officer and father have come in this section of town. Saving lives, arresting Dallas's only serial killer, and most important, the birth of my children at Methodist Central Hospital on Colorado and Beckley, are all unforgettable portraits permanently painted on my mind.

I met my wife in Oak Cliff. She lived on Clinton Avenue and we were married at the Disciples of Christ Church located at Brandon and Hampton. I've spent many summer afternoons monitoring traffic at Clarendon and Marlborough while trying to beat the heat by consuming the world's best snow cones at Aunt Stelle's.

As in my Police Perspective column, I will stay true to my loyal readers by providing an unfiltered look into the past, a moment in time that—good, bad or ugly—shaped who we are today as individuals and a community. The rough times of record-setting homicides and gang violence led to a new way of policing which helped to revitalize a decaying community and opened the door for opportunity. Drive around Oak Cliff today and the signs of revitalization cannot be mistaken.

But in my day. . .

Crime and Violence

What would a book about stories from the street be without crime and violence? Other than empty and extremely boring, and my days in the Hidden City were neither. Other officers I meet across the country can't fathom how, at the height of gang violence, I responded to seven shootings during one eight-hour shift, or how we used to pull into brick car washes or covered parking garages on New Year's Eve just to avoid the shower of falling shrapnel from thousands of bullets being fired into the air.

During my years in Dallas we had a record-shattering number of murders, a serial killer who hunted women and cut their eyes out, and more than our fair number of officers who paid the ultimate price for protecting and serving the citizens of the city. Sometimes we won the battles, and I tried to pay particular attention to those small victories, but other times we simply lived to fight another day. Describing the sordid details of a single crime would fill a book, and the sheer number of offenses committed on my beat during these years could make an entire library bulge at its seams.

Here from the archives of Police Perspective are a few of my stories of crime and violence on the beat.

Robbery Averted

My eyes shift between cars, buildings, parking lots, and alleyways, a habit I have practiced thousands of times in order to keep my partner and me alive. This intersection is one of the busiest in the city, and where others see a freshly painted convenience store, my mind flashes back to two black males getting off of the bus near the 7-11.

They headed directly to the alleyway without once looking toward the store. It didn't seem natural. (It reminded me of the times a kid will intentionally look away from his parents because he knows if he looks them in the eyes they will realize he is up to no good). They were both carrying what looked like small duffel bags as they made their way around to the side of the building, where they disappeared from sight.

A few years ago the store's owners were fighting the city about a right-of-way, and were allowed to put up a fence. Anyone familiar with the area knew that the alley was a dead end, and anyone at the mouth of the alley would quickly see that it didn't go anywhere.

"Something's wrong," I told my partner as we stealthily made our way around the back of the store, crawling over trash and around the fence which was now partially collapsed. We were only about 30 feet away and had the tactical advantage, because the open side of the alley was also the side that collected all of the noise from vehicles on the adjacent street.

We could see them now. Like dogs digging in the trash, they were engrossed in their task and totally oblivious to anything around them. From our vantage point it appeared that both of the men were bending down looking at something, taking items from the bags, but our view was obstructed by their bodies.

Suddenly they shifted positions and I could see they were loading weapons, two black semi-automatics. I heard the distinct sound of a magazine snapping into place and the chambering of a round. I could see them talking to each other and motioning as they pulled something else from their bags.

With our weapons drawn and at the ready, we waited to make our move. Now I could see two black masks being pulled from the bags, and knew what was next. We would have only a split second to act, but it might just be enough. As the two would-be robbers laid their guns on the ground in order to pull their black ski masks over their faces, I yelled to my partner "Go!" and we raced forward with guns drawn.

"Police!" "Freeze!" I yelled, "or I'll blow your ****ing head right off!" Within a split second we were all over them. The barrel of my Sig Sauer 226 9mm pressed firmly against the back of one head, and the other guy flailed for a weapon that had been kicked out of his reach. Not daring to reach for their weapons and begging for me not to shoot, the two bad guys were taken into custody and the crime was over before it started.

Inside their duffel bags we found extra ammunition and day-long Dallas Area Rapid Transit (DART) bus passes. They also had bus schedules to tell them exactly how long it would be between buses. Their plan was apparently to ride the bus to the store, rob the store, and then take the next bus back home.

I think it was boxing champion Mike Tyson who once said, "Everyone has a good plan until they are hit in the mouth," and today we hit them in the mouth before they were able to hurt anyone. Not only were they going down for the having the weapons, but they were both convicted felons with a host of outstanding warrants.

On the way to jail I tried to lift their spirits by telling them at least they didn't have to take the bus home.

Left for Dead

More often than not, it's the ghosts of crimes and criminals that dominate my thoughts and invade my dreams at night. Instead of feeling good about having found a missing two-year old who had been left on her own all night in the inner city by her mother's boyfriend, my mind gravitates to the negative side of the story.

Apparently, the boyfriend had become disenchanted with the relationship. The couple had a fight and he killed her, leaving her in the house and taking her preteen son and toddler daughter. After driving around for several hours in her stolen car, he decided that witnesses were not a good idea. He killed the son, leaving his body in a field and simply abandoning the baby in the middle of the night on an evening when the temperatures dipped near freezing. After the sun rose the next morning someone saw the baby wandering the street in the frigid weather, wearing just a set of toddler clothes over her diaper—no coat, hat, or mittens.

My partner and I responded to the call and within minutes had secured the freezing child. I removed my heavy police jacket and placed it around her and placed her in the car, called for an ambulance and advised the youth division to start looking for the parents.

As we waited for the paramedics I checked the toddler and noticed no visible signs of trauma such as cuts or bruises, but something was strange about her clothes. She did not look like many of the children in this neighborhood who wore tattered clothes or obviously well-used hand-me-downs. She had a typical outfit for a two-year-old, but she wasn't dressed for the outdoors. If her parent was concerned and caring enough to dress her in a cute outfit but not give her a coat or hat, I began to surmise that maybe the parent didn't know she was going to be outside. That led me to think something had happened unexpectedly to the parent.

I was starting to get a really bad feeling about this call.

With the paramedics now removing my jacket from the little girl and checking on her, I noticed something I missed on my original examination for injuries. I saw that her clothes were dirty but only on one side, as if she had been lying on the ground. I stepped forward to have a closer look at the dirt, and quickly realized that the dirt and grass mixture was being held together with what appeared to be a dried, brownish substance that I had seen all too many times before. The little girl had been lying on the ground, maybe sleeping in a pool of blood. Since she had no injuries, the picture of the events of the previous night involving this toddler, and maybe her parent, had suddenly become gruesome.

As the paramedics completed their medical evaluation, confirming no injuries but possible hyperthermia from the night out in the cold, our search of the area revealed that the "Found Child" call would indeed morph into a homicide, for we discovered the deceased body of her brother lying in a nearby field. Even more heart-wrenching was our discovery of the cleared spot on the ground marking the location where the child spent the night snuggled up to her dead or dying brother. Maybe his last act on this earth, as his life dwindled away, was providing just enough body heat to keep his baby sister alive.

Basket Case

Not long ago I was sitting with my son on the floor playing cops and robbers with his toy men, and he hid one of his guys in a wicker laundry basket that holds his dirty clothes. The game was innocent enough; little did he know when he tried to fool me that it wasn't the first time I had searched a similar basket.

As I pulled the top off of his clothes basket in an effort to reveal the hidden treasure, my mind flashed to a dark and cold December night on the street.

The dispatcher was asking for anyone in the area to assist the Fugitive Unit in searching for a cop killer in the area. Apparently this individual had killed a police officer in Louisiana and fled to our fair city. We had a vague description of the suspect, but it struck me at the time that we were searching for a needle in a haystack without a specific area to search in, or a good photo of the suspect. The Fugitive Unit had been setting up on the suspect's car but spooked him before he could get back to it, and he fled on foot. The pursuing officers had lost him in a maze of interconnecting apartment complexes, and called for help from the beat officers.

As I made my way through the dimly lit apartment complex I continually scanned the horizon in front of me, looking for anything that appeared out of place. Since I was not intimately familiar with the complex or its residents, the search was futile.

After more than an hour, most of the other officers had given up and cleared the area.

I had worked up an appetite, and in keeping with the great eating habits I had developed working the streets, decided that even though it was freezing outside I would grab an ice cream at a nearby convenience store. As I satiated my hunger I began to ponder where the suspect might have gone. I knew from my years of hunting that often when several hunters were in the woods together the animals would scatter and hide, but once it got quiet again they would continue their never-ending search for food, water or a place to safely rest. I wondered if humans exhibited the same traits. I wondered if I went back into the apartment complex by myself, might the suspect have resurfaced, especially if he thought the coast was clear and all of the officers were gone.

I had never tried this tactic before, but at least it would give me something to do on this cold evening.

My ice cream cone was almost gone, so I decided to give it a shot. Leaving my squad car in the parking lot, I crossed a street and set of railroad tracks and began walking and stalking through the apartment complex. Silently I made my way in and out of corridors, between buildings, and around parking lots, but my hunt was to no avail. I thought to myself that it had been a silly idea in the first place; since man is so much more evolved than animals, of course my postulation was preposterous.

Just as I was about the leave the property, feeling happy that I had not shared my idea with any other officers (and thereby avoiding an evening full of ridicule from my peers), a "suspicious person" call was received from the apartment complex just doors away from my present location. I jumped on it and told the dispatcher I was already at the location, and asked her to read the call's comments.

She told me the complainant had heard noises coming from her first floor patio and was frightened. Within seconds I was peering onto the patio from behind an adjacent wall. I shined the light from my flashlight around the small porch. The siding glass door appeared closed and locked, and no one was in sight. Everything seemed to be in its place. All of the potted plants were in order, and a bicycle was still chained to the large outdoor grill to prevent either item from wandering off in the middle of the night or whenever its owner was away.

As I continued to scan the patio and moved closer to check the back door, the beam from my flashlight illuminated a large wicker basket. Although its top was firmly in place, the container was certainly large enough to hold a small man. Since I had no idea what size the bad guy was, my mind convinced me that the suspect could be inside. So with my oversized voice I shouted, "Take the top of the basket off slowly, or you're going to die in that basket tonight – NOW!" I yelled, as my flashlight lit up the basket and its unknown contents. Just as I was thinking that I was never going to hear the end of it if my cover shows up and spies me yelling to a basket of trash or leaves, the top began to move.

"Slowly!" I yelled, but I was scared now and my voice cracked. I hoped he didn't notice that because it might give him a psychological advantage.

"Slowly, hands up," I yelled, attempting to regain my commanding voice, but not sure if I accomplished it. By now his hands were fully exposed and I saw no weapon. But this guy had already killed one cop, and I worried that he wouldn't hesitate to kill another if he had the chance. I needed to buy time for either my cover to reach me or to figure out what my next move was.

Now his arms were all the way out of the basket and he paused, waiting for my next command. With no backup there yet, I wondered what I was to do.

"Listen: I want you to push the basket onto the ground and keep your arms extended where I can see them!" I yelled. I thought if I could get him into an off-balance position I might have a chance to get close enough to handcuff him. But as he began to push the basket to the ground, I realized I had a problem: what was I to do with my hands? I had a gun in one hand and a flashlight in the other, and still had to reach for my handcuffs and then be able to get over to him to secure him without giving up my tactical advantage.

My mind was still spinning when the seemingly unsolvable conundrum was solved for me, as the apartment owner turned the porch light on. Apparently, she had heard my verbal commands to the suspect and wanted to see what was happening on her patio. The newly lit porch was exactly what I needed; in an instant my flashlight was in my pocket, and I had control of my handcuffs.

As the basketed suspect hit the ground I was on him, grabbing his hands and cuffing them together while still ready to pop a cap in his head if he even flinched. Thankfully for both of us, he didn't and I didn't. By the time my cover got there he was in custody. The other officers asked me why my squad car wasn't in the parking lot. As a matter of fact, they noticed that it wasn't even in the apartments.

"Long story," I said as we placed the murder suspect in the back of their car and began our short trip to jail and the suspect's long extradition back to Louisiana to face capital murder charges.

About that time my son snapped me back to reality by asking, "How did you know the toy was in the basket?"

"Isn't that where all bad guys hide?" I replied.

He looked confused and didn't know what to say.

"It's a long story - maybe I'll tell you sometime. Right now I feel like some ice cream. What about you?"

Worthless Parents

Since I have donned the badge and taken the oath, I have been upset, enraged, outraged and infuriated and at times mad as hell, but nothing has made my blood boil as much as a woman and her children did the other day.

Of all the individuals I have come in contact with over the years, this woman had the audacity to display her disrespect for authority and lack of morals and values in front of not only the police, but her own children. As a matter of fact, she delved even further into the world of aberrant behavior as she blatantly instructed her children to first steal, then lie, and finally to perform an act for the police so convincing that Hollywood agents should come calling any day now.

Allow me to regress a moment since I am so upset the words are pouring from my brain faster than my pen can write.

A few days ago, my partner and I were called to a store to arrest a shoplifter. Once inside we observed a woman and two small children. The woman had been caught stealing and as we proceeded to arrest her, the children, ages 4 and 6, started to cry and beg for us not to take their mother away.

They told us their father abused and beat them and they never had any food or money. The two girls cried and wailed and hung onto the legs of their mother, who pleaded that she was not stealing for herself but for her impoverished daughters.

This scene was so emotional that all the officers in the store were choked up and second-guessing our actions. The owner of the store finally could not take this heart-breaking scene any longer and, as we prepared to take the mother to jail and the children to Child Welfare, she interrupted and said she did not want to press charges. Her conscience could not stand the thought of those children all alone at Child Welfare.

An agreement was reached between the woman and the owner, and without delay we transported the entire family to a woman's shelter where they would be cared for by the devoted staff.

No sooner had we returned to our office than the phone was ringing off the hook. On the other end was one of the counselors from the shelter with incredible news.

Apparently she had talked with the two precious little girls and discovered that their whining and wailing at the store was just an act, and that they had been taught to do that if their mother was ever caught stealing. The counselor learned that these girls had been through this routine countless times and their mother had trained them what to do and how to act to gain the sympathy of a store owner and the police. The girls said they had used this act on many occasions to help their mother steal.

The whole episode was a con game and we had been fooled by a pair of professional-acting children. I was and still am furious. I cannot imagine what kind of parents would teach their children to steal and lie to cover up their own criminal activity.

I often have complained about parents who play ostrich and keep their heads in the sand when it comes to seeing their offspring commit criminal activities, but this case beats them all.

There is no excuse for this type of behavior and I would love to attend a repeat performance by the two children, because I guarantee instead of applause at the end of the show, one would hear only the sound of metal handcuffs being closed around the wrists of a parent who should lose her title as mom.

Smell of Death

I can remember being called time after time to the Medical Examiner's Office at Parkland Hospital. Parking on the side just off the emergency room entrance, making my way through the door marked with a sign stating "Authorized Personnel Only." I would walk down the hallway, making my way toward the cold grey steel doors of the elevator used to move the bodies from the hospital upstairs—with the living—to the morgue located below, where far more bodies are horizontal than vertical.

As the elevator makes its way down, the smell is there, but faint like background music in an elevator: you know the music is playing, but you're not really paying attention to it. Suddenly, the archaic elevator comes to an abrupt halt and the doors open slowly, as if the elevator itself is struggling for its last gasps of life.

As soon as the doors part, it hits you. The unique smell of the combination of cleaning solution and death is unmistakable. I would shake my head instinctively as if to try to shake the smell from my nostrils, to no avail. Not only was the smell in my nose, but it seemed that it was there to stay, permanently embedded, and forever reminding me of this place.

As I made my way into the holding area where bodies are placed before the autopsy, it was as if I'd stepped into everyone's worst nightmare, or some freaky "Ripley's Believe It or Not" special exhibit on Hell. Cold, dead bodies on every table were scattered around the room in no apparent organization. Old bodies in nightgowns; people who died unattended; young bodies in party dresses, the victims of a drunk driver. Good people and bad people, victims and criminals, all thrown together in this cold, dark room. Many of them were still dressed in bloody clothing, with knives protruding from their torsos; some with obvious gunshot wounds to the head, dried blood pooled in their hair, or with tubes and gauze still in place from valiant attempts by ambulance crews to save their lives.

On busy holiday nights, or on weekends, bodies fill the room to capacity, leaving little space to navigate around the freshly dead, and tasking doctors and their medical assistants ("dieners") to the limit. Since Parkland is the County hospital for Dallas, the morgue is utilized not only by this city of one million-plus residents but by the entire County of more than thirty municipalities.

When standing among the dead, you feel as if those ghastly images will be burned inside your brain forever, but—as with a childhood pet or lost young love—they fade with time. But the smell, the combination of death and cleaning agents, is one memory I've never ever been able to shake.

Headless

I look to the west down Colorado Boulevard and remember the search for a headless motorcycle rider.

The young man had been driving too fast, hit a patch of wet road, and laid the bike over before crashing into a telephone pole. Now, officers had a broken and battered cherry-red TNK race style, street legal 250cc motorcycle with all the bells and whistles any rich kid could ask for — as well as the body of a young white male wearing a matching cherry red leather motorcycle jacket and pants, but with no head. His body had been thrown from the motorcycle, and either the way he struck the pole, or its supporting guide wire, severed his head from his body, causing the head to fly off in an unknown direction.

Talk about a morbid job sometimes. It's bad enough working a bloody fatal accident, but now trying to find the head just exacerbates the situation. You can just imagine the 'headless horseman' type jokes as officers searched. I think I remember telling the story of another wreck I worked years earlier when a young woman was thrown through the window of her car and struck the rear of a moving company van which had fled the scene. We had a vague description of the rented van but no license plate number to positively identify the vehicle. At least we didn't think we had a license plate number — until we turned over the woman's body to discover the actual license plate embedded on her forehead...case closed.

We eventually found the young man's head inside the helmet, an incredible distance from the accident scene. Apparently when it separated from the body it had rolled down the hill, across a street, jumped a curb and finally rested in the manicured front yard of a north Oak Cliff residence.

Hard as I try, I can't erase the image of one of my fellow officers walking up Colorado holding that cherry red helmet with a severed head still strapped inside the protective case.

Even worse, I can still hear the grizzled veteran saying, "Alas, poor Yorick, I knew him well."

Blink of an Eye

I think to myself how quickly your entire life can change. But it's no different here than out on the streets. One moment you have your whole life ahead of you, and the next. . .

My mind flashes to just after 1:00 a.m. on a Sunday morning not very far from the place I'm sitting right now.

The heat was still lingering in the air from the scorching day just completed. The temperature was unpleasant, but the humidity made the evening almost unbearable. In this section of Dallas County, air conditioners were still a luxury item, and most of the $100-a-week apartments which proliferate in the area were lucky to have a fan to circulate the hot damp air.

On this night an air conditioner would have been a true blessing, because Mother Nature was not providing even the slightest hint of a breeze. As most officers are well aware, when the weather is unpleasant it seems that tempers begin to flare and patience is worn threadbare far sooner than normal. If the weather was any indication, this night had all of the makings of a deadly evening.

As two of the officers assigned to work the special Violent Crimes Task Force, my partner and I realized that if we made it through a full shift without any aggravated offenses it would be a miracle. With less than one hour to go before calling it a night and heading home, we commented on how we had not even answered a single "shots fired" call, let alone a family fight (a "domestic disturbance" to the police). Even though it was the weekend of a pay period, hot and uncomfortable, and one in which a large number of people were milling around drinking and partying, maybe our luck was going to hold out this time, maybe we had misjudged the evening. Sometimes we become jaded and expect the worst.

And sometimes. . . it happens.

Not a minute after our conversation, the night took an ugly turn, as the dispatcher blared out a disturbance call and then, seconds later, upgraded the fight to a shooting. By the time the first officers arrived, it was mayhem in the apartment complex; a young woman lay dead, her body sprawled in the dirt, with a single gunshot wound to the face.

Within minutes, sirens screamed through the night air and the flashing lights of squad cars illuminated the neighborhood as the search for the killer was on. Officers were busy establishing a crime scene, talking to witnesses, comforting the family, and trying to track down the mysterious assailant who only moments before had been seen talking with his victim.

As my partner and I guarded the corpse, the situation was rapidly brought under control. We once again realized just how oppressive the night air had become, as we both were sweating profusely and privately cussing our dismal situation. The mosquitoes were striking our arms and legs as if we were in the Everglades instead of Dallas, and the combination of heat and humidity was quickly sapping us of our energy. We recalled that just a few minutes earlier, we had been commenting on the calm of the evening; now we were face-to-face with the violence of the night.

"It is amazing," I thought out loud, "how fast things can change," to which my partner replied, "You think they changed for *us*? Do you think that just a few minutes ago she thought that she would be dead?"

Of course few of us think that the next moment could be our time to meet our Maker. We always feel that it is going to be the other guy, but that is not necessarily how it turns out. Nobody thinks today might be their last day—but what if it was? Are we living a life that we are proud of and would like others to remember us by? Would we do things differently if we knew this was going to be our last day? Would we be more compassionate, kind, and loving?

My partner was right. As I stared down at the motionless form of the murdered woman, I felt sure that she probably did not know that that day would be her last, and I was reminded again of just how abruptly life can end for any of us.

Murder Solved

One of the strangest cases that I ever worked involved a murder that had already been closed by our detectives and classified a suicide. On the night of the incident, I told them that I felt this was no suicide or accident. In my opinion, the position of the body on the ground, the distance from the wall, and, most important, the reports on the individual's positive demeanor even though he was terminally ill, just didn't add up to a suicide.

But what did I know? I was just a street cop.

A few days went by and I just could not get the case out of my head. It just didn't make sense to me that a guy who was probably going to die in a few months would take his own life by jumping off a four-story roof. Twenty stories, maybe, but four is really just a gamble on whether the fall would kill you or just cause further pain and agony.

Anyway, as has been my nature since the day I donned the badge (and if you ask my mother, since the day I was born), I persisted in asking questions and refused to just blindly accept the easy answer. So I kept digging and amazingly, without much effort, I soon discovered that the victim had indeed been fighting with another resident of the shelter. Asking a few more questions I soon discovered that the facility had recently installed security cameras, and within short order found the security footage of the victim and another man arguing and struggling on the staircase leading to the rooftop immediately preceding the incident.

Now, armed with a photo of the suspect, it didn't take long to ascertain what room he lived in. After a few knocks on the door he answered and told me he was just waiting to be arrested for his crime. He readily admitted to getting into a fight with the victim over some property and pushing him off the roof. Literally within minutes, the suspect voluntarily gave me a full confession. Maybe even stranger than him confessing was that he had no reason to confess since the case had been officially closed. Maybe he was just trying to clear his conscience before he too met his Maker, as he was also terminally ill and realized he wasn't going to live to see a trial or spend a day in prison for pushing his rival off the roof.

As has happened on multiple occasions during my career, I waltzed a prisoner into Homicide and said "Here is your murderer."

And once again, I'm still waiting on the thank you card.

A Stroll in the Park

I fondly remember that spring day on the corner of Colorado and Zang Boulevard where I helped to save a man's life.

Patrolling the park, my partner and I noticed a group from the senior citizens' center who had walked across the street to enjoy the afternoon. There must have been over two dozen gray Americans swapping stories and having a picnic on the lawn. I can't remember the occasion, but the nursing home staff had provided brightly colored decorations, plenty of food, and good times for everyone.

Well, almost everyone. During the festive outdoor celebration one of the participants began to choke, and lost consciousness. A crowd soon formed and instinctively my partner and I ran into the noisy confusion. Immediately noticing that the victim on the ground was not breathing, I performed a modified Heimlich maneuver, dislodging the food before beginning mouth-to-mouth resuscitation. The paramedics soon arrived, telling us that the man was lucky we were in the area and trained to help, or his trip to the park would have been anything but a picnic.

I received a letter from his family several weeks later thanking me and letting me know he had fully recovered and the city honored my partner and me with a lifesaving bar for our efforts.

Father and Son

There are sections of North Oak Cliff that are enchanting, with quiet tree-lined streets and old trees that can evoke memories of a bygone era. It's an area that has been in some type of gentrification for many years now, with brick cottages that were built in the 1940s immediately adjacent to rotting, wood frame homes with broken windows, missing doors and as much furniture outside on the porch as inside the house.

As we pass Denver approaching Marsalis Avenue, my heart rate increases and I feel the rapid beat in my chest. There is an uneasy feeling arising in my stomach. (I never was much for vomiting, which has been an asset in my line of work. Let's face it: no one wants to run up to a shooting victim or walk into a home where a loved one has just put a shotgun in their mouth, and lose their lunch all over the place). Thankfully, I get that queasy feeling for just a moment and then it goes away.

But now the queasy feeling returns and I know exactly why. I try not to look to my right because I know what I'm going to see. The same images I've seen every time I pass this intersection, and the same images that have come back to haunt me night after night for years now, images I just can't seem to shake. Then my head turns to the right--it's as if my mind refuses to let me forget, and forces me back in time.

I was just patrolling the neighborhood with my squad car windows down, enjoying the wonderful fall day. The kind of day where you relish the cool air after a long hot summer in a neighborhood where houses with window units still seem to outnumber those with central air conditioning. Just one of those precious Dallas days, where you love the feel of blue jeans, long sleeve shirts and cool air making your face tingle as the breeze whistles down the street and you finally feel like doing some of those outdoor chores that you have been delaying through those long dog days of summer.

I remember reveling in the autumn temperatures and watching one of the neighborhood dads working on a car with his toddler son. I was probably wishing I was home with my own boys as I watched the youngster lying down right next to his father, intently watching every move he made. When suddenly for some unknown reason, the jack slips and the car falls and I am forever cursed with the memory of the screams, the blood, and the unimaginable agony on the face of a dad as he sees his baby, his three-year-old, whose life is crushed under the weight of a fallen car. The father couldn't pick up the car. I couldn't pick up the car. The little one's life was ending on the driveway and there was nothing anyone could do about it.

A wonderful fall day no more.

Lessons Learned

Life on the streets is a constant learning process. Knowledge gained from each call for service helps you respond to the next, and often can be the difference between life and death. As in most occupations, knowledge is power. In law enforcement, senior officers (sometimes referred to as "Old Heads") are the informal leaders who in their own unique ways attempt to pass knowledge on to the younger generation. New officers also receive formalized instruction from Field Training Officers who spend months trying to prepare their young protégés. Both groups have different methods of instruction, but the goal is the same: to help young officers survive what the streets will constantly be throwing at them.

In this section I will try to relay just a few anecdotes that I have gathered over my years on the streets. Some of these tales I personally experienced, while other words of wisdom were passed on to me, and now I pass them on to you.

Ham

As I walk the streets of my beat searching for lawbreakers to incarcerate, I spend a great deal of time speaking to the good citizens of the area. I listen to their problems and try to hand out helpful hints to make their lives and my job a little easier. Hopefully they put their newfound knowledge to good use and do not become just another crime statistic. Many times, to my dismay, I hear the phrase, "But we have never done it that way!" My response is usually, "Well, maybe that is why you have the problems that you do."

At one establishment on my beat, the receptionist directs all service representatives and salesmen to the rear of the building to park. The rear parking lot is bordered by an alley and two small streets are adjacent on either side. In a span of just a couple of weeks, two vehicles were stolen from that unprotected rear parking lot. When I asked the receptionist about the visitors parking out front, or having a dock worker keep an eye on the vehicles parked in back, her response was the typical "Well, we have never done that before."

Being as long-winded as I am verbose, I decided to relate this little story that I trust would make an impression on the skeptical office worker:

It seems that several years ago at a huge family reunion down in the Hill Country, some four generations of mothers and daughters found themselves chit-chatting as they prepared a beautiful ham for the evening meal. At one point, the great-granddaughter of the clan asked her mother why she always cut an end off the ham before placing it in the oven.

Her mother promptly replied that she did not know why, other than that her own mother had always done it that way, and suggested that they should ask the grandmother. Both approached the grandmother and posed the question. After a moment of pondering, the grandmother answered that she did not know the reason, but that she had always done it that way. She suggested they ask the great-grandmother.

Now the matriarch of the family was approached and asked by the youngest member of the clan why they always cut the end of the ham off before cooking it. The great-grandmother responded that the only reason she did it was because she did not have a pan large enough to cook the entire ham.

I think you get the point. Just because it has not been done that way in the past does not mean we cannot blaze new territory. In crime fighting, if we find a better way for the citizens to protect themselves, or can offer suggestions to reduce crime, then it really does not matter if it has not been done that way before.

The perceptive receptionist got the message, and I hope so did all of you. The receptionist now has a rotating shift of dock workers keep an eye on the vehicles in the rear parking lot, and I have not taken another theft report since my last visit.

You know, the amazing fact is that they had never done it that way before.

Old Head

Zang and Illinois is not a bad intersection per se,
either direction and you could find apartments t
with roaches and drug dealers, both groups milling around in the
dark and hiding whenever lights are cast upon them.

As I turn the corner and head south on Zang, I spy the
apartments on the left and can't help but remember the time I
was travelling in this exact spot and some undercover officers
called out for help. They were chasing a wanted felon through
the apartment complex and needed some additional bodies.

As my car jumped the curb heading across the grass in
pursuit I glanced up to notice an "Old Head," a semi-affectionate
term for a veteran police officer. This one happened to be a real
dinosaur, an investigator who had been on the job since the
military released him from his tour of duty in Vietnam. I just kept
driving, figuring he was out on his way to lunch and wanted to
see how the real police work in the modern world. Heck, we even
have computers in our squad cars now, but I was sure he still
used a pen and pencil to fill out his reports.

The good guys were now chasing the bad guys on foot and
they were headed for the creek, so I decided I would cut them off
at the bridge, but when I slammed on the brakes over the rain-
swollen creek I saw that the Old Head was already there. A split
second later, the suspect had forded the creek and was running
on the other side.

I threw my car into gear and off I went to a dead-end street where the fugitive was sure to appear, but before I knew it he was heading into the nearby apartments.

"He is going into 1903!" I heard someone shout over the radio as I sped across the front yard of the complex, bailing out of my car and heading for the front entrance. No sooner did I arrive then I saw the Old Head now out of his car and standing by the front door.

By this time the cavalry had descended upon the apartment complex, as officers who had been chasing this felon in their cars and on foot were catching up and surrounding the building. Once officers had all possible escape routes blocked—doors, windows, fire escapes and maintenance crawl spaces—I gained entry to the apartment, followed by several other officers. Gun in hand, not knowing if the bad guy was really in the apartment, if he was armed and if he was going to shoot me, I moved cautiously through the small residence.

From living room to the kitchen and finally into the small bedroom I darted across hallways and behind door jambs, until I saw the figure of a large man hiding under a single sheet, sprawled out on the bed. Within seconds a half dozen officers joined me as I grabbed the suspect, quickly handcuffed him, and placed him under arrest. When I turned him over to talk to him, the first face he saw was not mine but that of the Old Head, to whom the bad guy cordially said, "Hello, I figured if I got caught again, you would be the one."

The Old Head did not respond. He simply removed the pen from his shirt pocket and waved it at the handcuffed prisoner. Everyone in the room knew what the signal meant. The Old Head had discovered years ago that the bad guys are more afraid of his pen than his gun. The weapon might kill you, but the pen will send you to prison, and this three-time loser was going to be gone for a very long time. The prisoner just shook his head at the veteran officer and quietly succumbed to his undeniable future.

As we cleared out of the building I noticed the Old Head walking by himself to his car. He was definitely older now, and more than a few pounds heavier than when he traded his green fatigues for a blue uniform and shiny badge. I thought, "He doesn't run much any more."

But when you are always one step ahead of the bad guy, I guess you don't have to.

First Day Jitters

The dynamic between the Old Heads and the young cops, and the training officers and their rookies, is a unique one that to many outsiders may appear rough or even cruel sometimes. The senior officers are responsible for maintaining their regular workload of trying to keep the streets safe, as well as for teaching and molding the young officers and, at the same time, just trying to keep both themselves and their young urban warriors alive. Any one of these tasks alone could drive a normal person crazy, yet these unsung heroes perform their thankless tasks day in and day out.

Even though it might seem that senior officers are hard on rookies, this toughening-up period is really just another way of preparing them for life on the streets. I distinctly remember speaking very harshly to a young female recruit one time and warning her how any call on the streets could be her last, how one must pay attention at all times and how even the routine calls, if not handled properly, could turn deadly in the blink of an eye. Like most wet-behind-the-ear rookies, she looked at me like "yeah, yeah, old man, they told us all of that stuff in the police academy, so why don't you just save your breath and let me get to work."

Minutes later on her very first call, an accident on a busy boulevard, she was so focused on the wreck that she forgot that she was in the middle of a busy intersection; at the last possible moment I pulled her from in front of a speeding vehicle, which surely would have ended her new career if not her life. As I held onto her shirt and the top of her vest she was still and almost white as a ghost from her near-death experience, and I quietly whispered, "Every call can be your last. Pay attention."

With those few choice words of advice I pointed her back in the direction of the accident because, in spite of what just happened, she still had a job to do.

Funny thing about this profession: no matter how tired, scared, upset, or depressed you are, in the end you still have to serve the citizens you have sworn to protect.

Wrong Way Arrest

Now, don't get me wrong, not every rookie's first day on the job is almost their last. As a matter of fact, they are usually funnier than fatal, and for all of the senior officers out there it usually bodes well for us to remember that we were all rookies once and all had our fair share of follies.

I hadn't been on the streets long myself when I received a call I'll never forget. I was assigned to my usual sector (a geographical area of the patrol division) and so I was already somewhat familiar with where to drive and how to get around (though my MAPSCO with its detailed city street maps was never far away). I figured I would make a few traffic stops, maybe write a ticket to try to ease into the routine of finally being on my own, when a call came over the radio for me. It wasn't just any call; no, of course I couldn't start off like everyone else with a "take the report of a stolen bicycle" call, or "meet the lady at the diner regarding her missing toy poodle," but this was an in-progress priority call, the kind preceded by three beeps to get your attention.

The call was a robbery-in-progress at a liquor store. It was a store I'd never been to in my life, and I only had a general idea of its location. I had never worked in that sector of the division during my training, and only vaguely knew my way around. To make matters worse, my cover (the other squad car assigned to the call with me) told the dispatcher, "10-4, but be advised I'm coming from a long way off in heavy traffic. The loose translation was "It's going to take me forever to get there, so you're on your own, rookie."

I responded with the standard "10-4: I'm en route." I don't remember anything other than thinking here it is, my first call--an armed robbery in progress at a liquor store--and my cover is a million miles away and I have no idea where I'm going.

"Great way to start a career," I thought to myself, as I switched on the lights and siren, standard procedure when responding to robbery-in-progress calls. I made my way south in the general direction. The liquor store was less than three miles away, but because I did not know how to get there it seemed that it took forever. I finally turned a corner and saw the giant sign marking its location and felt relieved.

"I can't believe I found it," was my first thought, followed by "I sure hope the bad guy is gone by now." My relief was as fleeting as my thoughts, because I suddenly realized that I could not reach the liquor store from the street I was driving on, because right by the store the intersection split, and the liquor store was actually on a one-way street going the opposite direction from the way I was traveling.

I panicked. I couldn't remember if it was against departmental policy to drive the wrong way on a one-way if you're in a marked squad car and responding to a call. I didn't know what to do. Making my way around the entire block, even with lights flashing and sirens blazing, would take an eternity. I couldn't let the other officer (who had told the dispatcher and the entire listening world that he was miles away from the call) beat me to the scene--I would never hear the end of it. I would probably be disciplined, maybe even fired, because I couldn't find my way to my first call, and lives might be in jeopardy.

I was a basket case. I knew I had to make a decision on the one-way street, but didn't know what to do, and seconds were ticking away. The siren was loud and people around were looking at me, so I pulled my car into an alleyway and decided that I would run to the liquor store. All of the police academy training was instantly out the window, all of my field training program up in smoke, all of my senior officer patrolling gone, as I threw the car into Park and prepared to run to the scene of the crime.

Jumping from my vehicle and pulling my Smith & Wesson .357-caliber Magnum from my holster, I ran down the alley and headed toward the liquor store. I had no sooner rounded the corner out of the alley when kerpow! Just as in the Batman comics, I was knocked to the ground. Briefly stunned and a little dazed, I thought I had run literally into the proverbial brick wall, but then I looked up and saw someone else sprawled out and stunned on the ground. My gun had fallen out of my hand during the collision and I quickly reached for it, then noticed another gun, and a stack of bills being scattered by the breeze.

"Could this be. . .?" I wondered, as I quickly moved to jump on top of the bad guy and cuffed him.

About that time my other responding officer showed up and ran toward us. Within seconds the liquor store owner was at the scene, pointing at the guy on the ground and yelling, "That's the guy who robbed me!"

"Good job, rookie," said the senior officer, as he placed the robber in the back of my squad car. To this day I wonder if he was curious as to why my squad car was in the alley rather than in front of the liquor store where an officer would usually park. But he never asked and I never said anything about my hilarious—and obviously blessed—rookie mistake.

Air One

As a Field Training Officer, you try to expose your new recruits to as many different aspects of policing as possible, which often includes patrolling by car, boat, or air, depending on where you are assigned. With many options to choose from, my rookie had been hounding me about going for a ride in a police helicopter. He had heard from many of his classmates how exciting it was. He had heard how fascinating the view was from above as you search the ground for missing children, or follow suspects as they try to elude the police hundreds of feet below.

Actually, on his first day with me, I had arranged for a ride in the Dallas Police whirlybird, but a call about a fight in the neighborhood and a woman with a knife led us north to jail instead of south to Redbird Airport where Air One is based.

Now, after much pleading from my young protégé, I once again called the Helicopter Section and begged that they take him for a ride so he could get this "helicopter business" out of his system and get back to the basics of learning his job as a street cop.

Fortunately, the pilots said that the evening was clear and they would be glad to take him up on their regular evening patrol, and even invited me to tag along if I so desired.

I had been up several times before, and although the scenery is nice flying so high with your head in the sky, I told the pilot a resounding "maybe," as I reserved that decision for later, hedging my bets that it might once again get busy on the street.

The night remained quiet, and after arriving at the airport I decided "What the heck! Going up for an hour can't be any more boring than waiting around down here," so I joined my rookie for the mandatory preflight safety briefing.

After a few minutes of cautions ("always enter and exit by the front of the aircraft," "keep your head low as you walk in and out," "wear your seat belt at all times," and "stay in your seat even in the event of an emergency landing—unless you see the pilot bail out, and then run like the wind!") before I knew it, we were airborne over Oak Cliff.

The patrol began exactly as billed, and just like all the other air patrols I had attended, was routine. We flew over our beat and checked out some known drop locations for stolen cars; we made a spin around downtown, feeling the turbulence that swirls in and out of these huge structures that make up our famous skyline. Next we proceeded to hit each one of the patrol divisions, eavesdropping on their conversations and spying their nightly activities from a protected distance far above their heads.

Then, as police work is famous for, a mundane patrol suddenly exploded into action as an Oak Cliff ICP element spotted a stolen car which was taken in a carjacking—and yes, the chase was on. Down I-30 heading east and the suspects were not stopping, blared our police radio as the dispatchers asked Air One to join in the chase.

"Still eastbound heading into the Mixmaster," the police dispatcher advised, as our pilot whirled the helicopter around and headed toward the chase.

Within a minute Air One was over the fleeing suspects, and we had a view of both the bad guys and the good guys chasing them as the cars sped down I-30. Time to "light them up," as two other squads pulled into position, and Air One hit the spotlight, letting the suspects know that they could run but could not hide from this eye in the sky. In an instant, the suspects pulled off the highway and the vehicle came to a stop.

As the officers bailed out to arrest them—wow! The chase was back on as the stolen vehicle once again sped away, and this time the pilot did a maneuver that took the copter nearly straight down on top of the suspects, in a move that turned my rookie's face white and gave him a memory he never will forget. With the helicopter now momentarily the only one in the chase, Air One was calling out directions as patrol cars tried to catch up to the fleeing suspects.

The vehicle went down Jim Miller and through some red lights, still going straight, which allowed the squads to catch up; now with patrol officers once again in pursuit, the stolen car made a hard right onto a side street, but Air One was still on top of them, into a dead end and around the horseshoe. Officers once again prepared to stop the suspects, but from the air we could see a body being thrown out of the vehicle—and yet the bad guys kept going and the radio traffic became even crazier, with officers shouting for ambulances for the wounded party.

And still the chase continued.

Now, out onto the main road again, but never out of the spotlight of Air One as the pilot did a magnificent job of flying and the co-pilot followed the suspects' moves and read out the streets on the MAPSCO at the same time. Out onto a long straightaway, and it looked like the stolen car was going to get away because the chase officers had to slow down to avoid accidents and flying bodies, but the suspects simply could not outrun the spotlight of the helicopter.

Suddenly, the driver punched the gas in an attempt to accelerate away from the cops, but he fishtailed and lost it, striking the center median and ripping off his rear wheel. He was in trouble now, and within a few hundred yards had no choice but to come crashing to a stop. Two more people bailed out of the stolen vehicle, right into the arms of the police and into custody. The driver, however, was protected from the officers' line of sight by his own stolen vehicle, and took off across the street and into a field, with no officers around.

Down a tree line, past a power plant, the driver continued, through some trees, over a few fences, and across a back yard or two, and no police in sight—except, of course, for Air One which had circled the area continuously and kept the suspect in the spotlight the entire time while guiding ground officers closer to his location. Masterful piloting and excellent co-piloting made all the difference in the world.

This suspect would have gotten away (at least for the time being) if it hadn't been for Air One, but after about a five-minute ground chase he realized he could not outrun the spotlight no matter how hard he tried. In exhaustion, he ran out onto a main street where he laid on the ground and promptly was placed into custody.

The good guys won, the bad guys lost, a great chase, lasting memories, and phenomenal flying. I'm glad I hadn't just stayed on the ground for another boring car chase.

Maslow

Although nowadays I make regular appearances as a law enforcement analyst for both the CNN and FOX television networks, the radio business has always near and dear to my heart. Thanks to Michael Spears, a former CBS radio executive, I had the unique opportunity to host a weekly talk show on KRLD, the local CBS affiliate. Those were some of the happiest days of my life. Working the streets, hosting a popular radio show and making guest appearances on the local FOX television station, fed my ego as I shared words of law enforcement wisdom each week.

My radio show, *Legal Eagles*, originated from the KRLD and Texas State Network studios located in the Ballpark in Arlington, home of the Texas Rangers major league baseball team. On more than one occasion my kids and I would get to the station early and make our way through the private entrances into the ballpark, long before fans were allowed inside, and sit and visit with the players. I remember my oldest son, David, a budding baseball player himself, sitting and talking with Bucky Dent, a Rangers coach and former Yankees Worlds Series hero. I remember my daughter Megan getting an autograph from Bobby Witt and some pitchers who were warming up in the bullpen but who took time to sign a ball and toss it up to the beautiful brown-haired, brown-eyed girl who hovered above them watching their every move. I remember my son Mark who protested once when I said I needed to go inside to prepare for my show, "But Dad, I hear you all day long! I'm playing catch with Rusty Greer," a promising young player at that time who went on to be immortalized in the Rangers Hall of Fame.

The Ballpark—or at least the radio station—also served as the place where my wife and I kind of had our first date. I say "kind of" because actually I was hosting my show and had invited some rookies from the police academy to come to the studio and have a chance to be on the air talking about what it was like to be in the Dallas Police Academy.

The idea for that particular segment of my weekly show had come to me a few days earlier when I made one of my frequent trips to the academy to teach this latest group of raw rookies, looking to be turned into streetwise cops. On that trip to the academy I was reunited with an old friend, Rex Post, a former colleague from the previous decade when we worked the Northwest Division, rounding up prostitutes and arresting drug dealers. He was assigned as the Class Advisor for this new bunch of rookies. He had to sit through all of the classes, monitor their work, read them the riot act whenever they needed it or violated some departmental policy or procedure, and even work out with them running the track and performing daily PT (physical training).

Class Advisor wasn't the most sought-after job in the department, but since it was at least a seventeen-week assignment and a break from the monotony of day-to-day police work, many of the officers enjoyed it. The biggest benefit for many was the break from evenings or deep nights, because the majority of rookie school was 8 a.m. to 4 p.m. Monday through Friday. It was almost like a "real job" that real people have in the other world outside of law enforcement.

I had decided this was going to be one of my last classes at the academy, and had already found a replacement to deal with these kids so I could work. But I think Rex was genuinely happy to see me, and we spent a few minutes reminiscing about the "good old days" of law enforcement in Dallas. He couldn't resist telling a few war stories (that I had hoped would never be brought up again), and then introduced me to the class as DPD's resident celebrity: "the man who caught Dallas's only serial killer and then wrote an award-winning book about the tale, and who now hosts both a radio and television show." He really let me have it on the intro, while I just wanted to get this class over and get back to real police work. Finally, he said, "And here to teach you community policing is the Father of Community Policing in Dallas: JJ Matthews."

The class went fine with no unusual distractions, except for a few comments from Rex trying to goad me away from the curriculum and into some war stories.

No unusual distractions, that is, until I began my discussion of Abraham Maslow's Hierarchy of Needs.

In Maslow's popular 1956 book *Motivation and Personality*, he postulated that all people have the same basic needs, the most basic being the need for food and shelter for survival; then safety and security. Without getting too academic, I used the Hierarchy of Needs to demonstrate to these recruits that no matter where they were assigned and no matter what population they dealt with, people were people with the same basic needs. After pure survival, we the police provided for society's basic need to be safe and secure in their homes and with their families.

I went on to talk about the rest of the Hierarchy, when I noticed two female recruits talking in the back of the room. That's a definite "no-no" when an instructor (and senior officer) is addressing a class. I stopped speaking as Rex started to jump up and chastise the two for not only talking when I was speaking, but for interrupting his friend, no less. I could imagine "Dear Chief" letters as punishment, and lots of push-ups resulting from this violation.

But I was in a good mood after seeing Rex (and probably from knowing this would be my last appearance at the Academy), so I waved him off. Rex sat back down and I asked the two young ladies to share their thoughts with the class. The more vocal of the two quickly turned snitch on her shy friend, whom I asked about the conversation.

The tall pretty blonde told me that she had studied Maslow and thought I had the third need wrong. I assured her I was correct, and held up an article in my training materials documenting my statements. I told her the Third Level was love and belonging; she refuted my statement and said the Third

Level was sex. Giggles broke out in class, and Rex would have no more of this. I invited the recruit to check my documentation after class, and we moved forward with the lecture with no more interruptions or whispering.

After class the young lass and her classmate did approach and look over the materials. Not relinquishing her position, she at least acquiesced to the same concept but with different wording. Rex was at the table ready to pounce, but I quickly turned the conversation into an invitation for him and his two recruits to visit my radio show over the weekend. I thought maybe I could get some good audio from these two, and Rex and I could catch up. Everyone agreed, so I gave them directions and told them I would see them on Sunday afternoon at the studio.

I don't remember what happened to Rex, but he didn't show. The two recruits, however, made their way out there for the broadcast. Now, over the years I have had numerous guests in studio, but none had ever called me a few weeks later and asked me out on a date. Although Jill was shy, her girlfriends had talked her into calling me, and when I told her I had commitments to my children that I had to keep before I could go on a date, she later said that convinced her I was the right guy.

Funny, how life works sometimes: she chased me and I ended up winning.

Within a few weeks I was dating Jill, the beautiful girl who would change my world and provide me with more happiness than one person should be allowed to have.

Mental Health

For years my partner and I would joke that it seemed that the mentally ill from all over the area were being dropped off on our beat, until we discovered that that was exactly what was occurring. Twice a month, buses from the mental health hospitals would drop the mentally ill off at a major intersection where they were forced to find their ways to any of the numerous day care houses that were being paid to feed and house them. For many of these individuals this was a regular routine: released back into society with 21 days of medicine, no money, and only the clothes on their backs or whatever they could carry. The day houses were paid by the state to provide food and shelter, and told to make sure the individuals took their medicine.

Many of these houses were terrible at best, and some should have been condemned for their living conditions. Most provided the bare essentials called for in their contracts, others even less. I don't want to get onto my soapbox about the deplorable situation of the mentally ill in this country, but I did live with it on a daily basis. I saw firsthand how those who had lost their way in this world were on the streets by themselves with no money or identification, often left in a strange city with no transportation, and they were supposed to navigate a social services system that would take an Ivy League graduate to figure out. Our mental health system is blight on our society, but someone with much more influence than a cop would have to solve this enormous problem. For now, maybe I should just paint you a picture...

Crazy Smart

At a recent merchant meeting, several people expressed a concern about what seems to be a growing number of street people. These street people are not necessarily homeless, but are those who may have been turned away by our mental health institutions or are free to roam around each day and return to sleep at night.

Most of these individuals are not dangerous, at least not when they stay on their medication, but their personal habits can range from abnormal to appalling. For the most part, these individuals are not committing crimes, and yet the police receive dozens of calls each week to "do something" with them because they look unsightly or are acting strangely and scaring off customers from area businesses.

On a recent call of this nature, I was reminded of a story I heard long ago but that made such an impression on me that I think about it to this day.

It seems that a few years back, a very successful businessman from Tyler started courting the girl of his dreams, who lived in Dallas. As part of his amorous ritual every Friday night, he put on his best clothes and headed out for the big city. On one particular night, he found himself venturing out into the teeth of a typical Texas springtime thunderstorm, complete with torrents of rain and 50 mph winds. At the height of the thunderstorm, the young man's luck took a turn for the worse—he discovered that he had a flat tire. To make matters worse, he was stranded alone in the dark right in front of the Terrell State Mental Hospital.

Being a positive person, he tried to take all of this in stride and do what he could to make it to Dallas before the night was totally wasted. So our dapper lover removed his coat and tie and plunged into the pouring rain and lightning-filled darkness to change his tire. Like so many of us when called to play roadside mechanic, he succeeded in removing the tire; so as not to lose the lug nuts, he placed them into the hubcap which was lying on the ground. Well, as luck would have it on this fateful evening, a strong gust of wind blew the hubcap and its contents into a nearby ditch, and the contents soon disappeared downstream.

Now, with hope fading and no way to get his tire on the car, our hero sat squarely in a mud puddle, staring into the night and dreaming of his wonderful date which was not to be. Somewhere around the height of his discontent, the young man heard a voice behind him and when he turned, saw a man sticking his head out of the window of the state hospital.

"What's wrong?" yelled the man.

Having nothing to lose and time on his hands, the drenched young man explained his predicament.

The man in the hospital listened to the tale, and after a minute offered a suggestion to the young lover. He said, "Well, if I was in your place, I think I would take one lug nut off each of the other three wheels and place them on the wheel where the lug nuts are missing. That way, all four wheels will have three lug nuts and you will be able to make it to a service station where you can buy some more lug nuts."

The young man sat astonished. "What a great idea!" he screamed, and went right to work. As soon as the last tire was in place, the young man shouted, "Thank you!" to his hospitalized assistant. "For awhile I thought you were a patient."

"I am," replied the man leaning out of the window, to which he added, "I may be crazy, but I'm not stupid," at which point he closed the window and returned to his special life.

Henry

On yet another mental health call I was at a halfway house just down the street on North Marsalis Avenue. In the middle of the call, Henry, one of the mentally ill residents who had been involved in a mini-melee, decided to crawl underneath my squad car and announce to the world that if I wanted to take him to jail I would just have to drag him there. Upon hearing the proclamation, I promptly got back into my car, started it up and revved the engine, all the while yelling at Henry and telling him, "I get paid the same whether I drag you or drive you: the choice is yours." I was sure my little patrol ploy would work, but it was to no avail, as the man remained under my car and refused to cooperate. As a matter of fact, he began making sounds like my police siren as if to taunt me.

About that time, I heard Steve, another one of the house's occupants and a man I had dealt frequently over the years, yell to Henry, "You had better get out of there right now because that cop is crazier than both of us put together, and he'll drag your dead bloody body all the way into your cell."

Maybe my warning didn't carry much weight but Steve's apparently did, as Henry immediately rolled from under my car and placed his hands behind his back, begging me to drive him — not drag him — to jail.

ACME

I distinctly remember the time in the middle of my beat when I responded to a disturbance call at one of those mental health day centers.

Apparently two male residents were picking on one of the smaller and feebler occupants of the day home, but it was nothing that would rise to the level of a criminal offense, which is what I informed the Director of the complex. She asked if I could at least sit everyone down and talk to them, so I grudgingly agreed, fully aware that little good ever came from these sessions. Within a short time, she assembled the three men in her office and I read them the riot act about how if this behavior did not stop I was going to throw the two instigators in jail for the rest of their lives. . . so on and so on, whatever I made up at the time.

I thought that I had put the fear of God into them and the situation would be resolved, but the one piece of the puzzle I had overlooked was the fact that all three of them were mentally ill, and no matter what I said it just sounded like Charlie Brown's teachers talking to him: blah, blah, blah.

So, the next day at 3:00 in the afternoon, the first call out of the box was a return visit to the mental health center. Once again, I sat the offenders down and told them to stop fighting or I would have them moved to another house, where the only thing they would be fed morning, noon, and night was cold soup. Of course, one of the men chimed up that he loved cold soup, so again my brilliant scheme was foiled.

Failing to come up with any other wonderful suggestions, I pointed my finger and in a loud voice said to them, "I'd better not have to come back here again or you're both going to regret it." It was the best I could do at the time.

As I made my way out the door, the victim stopped me and asked in his meek voice, "What can I do about those mean men? They are both bigger than me and they won't stop hitting and kicking me."

I knew he was frustrated and looking for answers, so without thinking (and that's a key factor here) I said, "You know, if it was me I would wait until both of them are sleep and then knock them in the head." With that I headed out the door and back to "real" police calls.

As luck would have it I didn't receive another call at the house the entire shift, until the last call of the night. As a matter of fact, I was already headed to the station to sign out when I heard an ambulance dispatched to the now-familiar address on my beat.

I told the dispatcher I would handle it and I turned the car around. I was glad I did, because as soon as I walked in the door I realized what had happened. Standing in front of me was one of the paramedics holding a brick from the garden; next to him was the meek victim of the prior abuse; next to him was the Center's

Director; and sitting on the couch were the two bullies who were both receiving medical attention and both displaying the word "ACME" clearly stamped into their foreheads.

The paramedic turned to me and said, "You're not going to believe this, but this little guy here says some police officer told him to do this."

I shrugged my shoulders and replied, "Now *that's* crazy."

Peanut Butter

Another brawl on the street with a mentally ill woman started out as my responding to a domestic violence call. By the time I arrived, the wife was running naked around the front yard and shouting how beautiful she was.

Although she was indeed attractive, some of her beauty had been hidden by the flour, peanut butter, and jelly she was coated with. Apparently she had spread the ingredients around on the floor and rolled in them. When her husband and child attempted to intervene, she grabbed a large kitchen knife and came after them.

Now she was standing in the front yard exposed to her neighbors and everyone passing by. I had to figure out what to do with a naked mentally ill woman covered in flour, peanut butter, and jelly, and armed with a knife.

This was not a scenario that had been covered in the police academy.

As I waited for help to arrive, the lady asked me if she was pretty. I told her that she was the most beautiful woman I had ever seen. Suddenly she dropped the knife and quietly sat down on the ground. I told her that I would sit with her until the paramedics came to look at some of the wounds she had earlier inflicted on herself as she flailed around with the knife.

In a few moments my back-up arrived, along with the paramedics. I asked everyone to stay back as I sat with my new friend on the ground.

The paramedics gave us a blanket and I told the woman we were going to take a ride together. She agreed and let me place the handcuffs on her for safety reasons. Quietly she got in the car and we talked for a few moments. She said she loved me and wanted to marry me and told me that we were going to have beautiful babies together.

It was quite a special time until the other officer—a female— got in the back seat with her for the drive to the mental ward at the county hospital. As happens so many times in relationships, the sight of the other female was too much to take. The woman yelled, screamed and cussed up a storm as she kicked the back seat of the squad car, and told me in no uncertain terms that I was the scum of the earth and she hated me like all the men in her life. With that, our whirlwind relationship was over.

I should have known it would never have worked. Not just because she was crazy, but because I'm allergic to peanut butter.

Rookie Bull___

Not every encounter with the mentally ill was violent, but nearly all of them had the potential for violence, and when one is working alongside younger and more inexperienced officers almost anything can happen. On one particular night I had the opportunity to work with one of these young and enthusiastic officers. You have seen the type: fresh out of the academy, these guys and gals in blue who still feel they can make a difference, and who hit the streets each night giving it 100 percent.

These youthful protectors of society have not yet been hardened by the streets and the system, and have not cloaked themselves in cynicism, only going through the motions of doing their jobs. The majority of these officers look forward to wearing their uniforms each day and helping the citizens by putting criminals behind bars where they belong. For one who has spent over half of my life behind the badge, the experience of working with these fresh faces was not only exciting, but invigorating.

On this particular night we responded to a call regarding a mental patient who had assaulted his wife and eight-month-old baby. When my partner and I arrived, the man (who was considerably bigger than both of us) presented a very imposing figure. The wife stated he had not been taking his medicine and just seemed to "fly off the handle," striking her and knocking the baby to the floor.

The situation did not look good for making a quiet arrest and getting on with our business, but as the young officer quickly started spitting out penal code violations and police procedure (most of which I had not heard in years) he shifted the man's attention away from me. As soon as I realized the abusive husband and father was as confused about what the officer was saying as I was, I slipped around behind the man and quietly asked him to put his arms behind his back.

Dazed by the verbal assault of my partner, the man was not really paying attention to what he was doing, and silently acquiesced to my request. Once his hands were behind his back, I quickly handcuffed him and we were out the door and on the way to jail with not a single punch thrown by anyone.

As we drove, I commended my partner on his quick thinking.

"That was a great distraction," I said. "You even had me confused with all that mumbo-jumbo police stuff!"

"What are you talking about?" he asked. "I was just telling the guy all of that stuff they teach us in the academy. I didn't know you wanted to arrest him until you handcuffed him."

We just looked at each other a moment before I broke out laughing. "Whatever it takes," I exclaimed. "No one was hurt and the bad guy is going to jail," I said through a chuckle.

I love working with rookies.

Compass

One place familiar to all cops in The Cliff was the Mental Health and Mental Retardation (MHMR) day facility on Twelfth Street. As my partner disappeared into a counselor's office to discuss a problem involving one of their clients, I found myself standing in the lobby of the center with some half dozen "special needs" individuals staring at me, touching my uniform, and asking me questions about being a policeman. I felt nervous, a little anxious, and probably more uncomfortable than anything else. My feelings of inadequacy made me tense.

This spur-of-the-moment question and answer session should have been second nature to me, because I did this all the time at schools and civic meetings. Children and people of all ages seem to gravitate toward officers, and have an endless supply of questions for men and women in blue. There was nothing different about this spontaneous encounter, except that I was in a special needs facility. Being in such a place made me uneasy. But I smiled and answered their queries, while silently wishing my partner would hurry up so we could leave. It was getting hot inside, and I could feel beads of perspiration on my forehead, but I continued to answer the questions and to show them my Batman belt of police equipment.

About the time I realized my partner was not coming out any time soon, and debated whether I should make a break for the door, then "Whew," I thought, with a sigh of relief, as I spied a savior from my fears.

The young man in the white lab coat introduced himself as Peter and asked me, "You don't feel comfortable, do you?"

I told him that my Mom works with special-needs individuals all the time, but as for me, they just make me a little nervous.

"Don't worry," he said. "The feeling is natural, kind of like when you meet a physically challenged person and don't know how to respond. Let me see if I can help you understand," he continued.

"If you look at society like a point on a compass, then the average person might be facing due north, but where mentally handicapped individuals are concerned, most of them are just a little off, like maybe facing northwest, if that makes sense?" he asked.

"Now that you put it that way, it does," I responded to my new friend.

He went on to tell me that in places such as this center, the staff provides clients with training and helps them establish a daily routine, which is extremely important. He told me that a strict routine will teach the clients to take their medicine, eat the proper foods, and stay away from drugs and alcohol, all of which will help the individuals live a rather normal life and get their compass back to pointing north again. With the proper medication, diet, and a little extra attention, these special people can be productive members of society, Peter assured me.

Peter's verbal illustration was wonderful. I shook his hand and thanked him for helping me feel comfortable again. His insight and wisdom had helped me to comprehend a segment of our society which I had been leery about for quite some time.

About that time, my partner and the center's Director walked up and said they had taken care of the matter leading to the call. I told them of my conversation with Peter.

To my surprise, the Director grabbed Peter by the arm and escorted him down the hall as he asked, "Now Peter, you haven't been playing doctor again, have you?"

Peter turned around to see the astonished look on my face and said, "I never said *my* compass pointed straight north."

Hope

Whereas my wife has always been the "glass is half full" type of person, after over three decades of policing not only do I know the glass is half-empty, but I firmly believe someone stole the missing contents. More often than not, hope in the inner city seems as elusive and unrealistic as the dreams of countless youngsters seemingly sentenced to a life of despair by their missing-in-action parents.

As you can probably tell by now, many of my stories from the street are filled with violence and death, so when I see a glimmer of hope I feel compelled to write about it and, more important, pass it along to you. Armed with these tales, I hope that you don't just view the glass as half full, but see the true potential in everyone no matter their personal situation or environmental handicaps.

In this section I have compiled several stories of individuals who seem to have little or no chance in the world and yet, despite their grim circumstances, give all of us hope for the future.

Spirit of the Season

I absolutely love the spirit of Christmas. I am one of those people who cannot wait to celebrate this glorious time of the year. I enjoy watching all of those Christmas specials on television, especially the ones taped in the mountains where the snow is waist-deep and the only way to get around is in a sleigh.

Each year I eagerly anticipate that wonderful day when we can pull all of the decorations out of storage and turn our house into our own winter wonderland. As Christmas music softly sends the sounds of the season throughout the house, I barely have the words out of my mouth that the Christmas tree is securely in its stand before my children, who are as excited as their Dad, begin hanging all types of ornaments from the branches. After some garland is placed over the fireplace, a score of music boxes are strategically deployed in every room, and so many sparkling lights are placed on the tree that Paris would look like a dimly-lit back alley in comparison, I finally declare the Christmas spirit is here again.

With eggnog being ladled from the holiday punch bowl, I scurry to grab a few hastily-wrapped packages to place under the tree so the little ones will have something to look at, wonder about, and occasionally shake when Dad has left the room.

With family coming in from around the state and across the country to celebrate the blessed event, and my daughter edging her way in between her two brothers for that extra space on my lap, my heart is warm and all seems right with the world. . . until I am forced to leave my sterile little rural environment and return to work some of the poorest and most violent streets in the city.

Areas of the city where the Christmas spirit is just another fairy tale that children have been hearing from Mommy or Daddy; like, "Someday we will move into a real house with a white picket fence and a big backyard for you to play in and when you are hungry you can eat whatever you want because we have plenty of food."

I work in areas where there are few Christmas lights and even fewer presents. Gifts in this part of town are few and far between.

As Christmas draws closer and anticipation rises around my own home, I find my feelings of anxiety grow more intense as I make my way south of the river to begin yet another day behind the badge in a place where Christmas may never come. No time to play Christmas music over the loudspeaker as the calls keep piling up on our computer, a fight here and a robbery there, just a few more examples of the Christmas spirit being stolen from the community.

As the clock works its way toward midnight, there is just enough time on the shift for one more call, and the dispatcher sends us on a drive-by shooting. As I pull up in front of the small cracker box house which probably had been built some seven or eight decades ago, I notice there are no signs of the season, no

"Sleigh Parking Only" signs or Christmas lights to adorn this small wood-framed structure.

Inside, the house is cold and for the most part empty. A small couch which has seen better days, a broken table, and two folding chairs adorn the main living area. The only heat is provided by a small space heater, and I notice only about half of its coils glow red with traces of warmth.

But over in the far corner of the room, something catches my eye.

Turning my flashlight toward the object I see a small tree, barely a foot tall and skinny, but indeed a tree. Drawing nearer I make-out a strand of old lights wrapped around the tiny branches, and some popcorn strung together and loosely laid over a few small limbs of the evergreen.

As I kneel down for a closer inspection, the outline of four small children comes into view. Ranging in ages from 2 years old to about 6, the youngsters are standing on the fringes of darkness watching me marvel at their homemade creation.

For what seems like several minutes we just stare at each other, until one bold little girl who could have been no more than 3 makes her way toward me into the light. With dark hair, golden skin and a face as fresh as new-fallen snow, her innocent beauty radiates through her smudged face and faded pajamas.

Without a sound she approaches the tree and reaches down into a small cup which I have not even noticed near its base. As the sound of the metal cup on the wooden floor echoes through the empty house, the tiny tot pulls out a small piece of red and white peppermint—not a whole candy cane, mind you, or even an entire mint—this was just a chip of candy. Inspecting the treat for a moment and finally deeming it worthy, she hands it to me and said, "You can have this. We have lots."

Staring in amazement at this little miracle, I have to force my lips to utter a grateful "Thank you." Having dutifully been acknowledged, the girl returns to the darkness and safety of her siblings. For more than a moment, I just stare in amazement at the special gift which has been placed in my hand.

Until I realize that the present I have received was not so much in my hand as in my heart. As I staggered to stand up straight, it dawned on me that Christmas was not the lights and the decorations nor the eggnog and the parties. Christmas is not an object or a place, it is a feeling. It is giving and sharing and the spirit which unites us all.

I could not believe what was happening. Here of all places, a run-down shack, barely more than a barn, in one of the poorest sections of the city, I found the Christmas spirit in the gift of a child.

But then again, maybe that is exactly how it is supposed to be.

Sophia

As I struggle to push those positive thoughts to the front of my mind, I recall Sophia, a young Hispanic female who greeted me for years as I made my morning trek to the local 7-11 on my beat.

Like so many of her contemporaries, she had dropped out of school at age 14 to have a baby. On multiple occasions, she tried to return to school; but with no money, no husband, and a little one to care for and feed, she lied about her age and entered the workforce. Cleaning homes for what amounted to little more than pennies a day, she soon realized she would repeat the fate of her young mother as well as her mother's mother—who upon Sophia's birth earned her title of grandmother at the ripe "old" age of 35.

Sophia was determined to make a better life for herself and her baby. With the resolve of a prizefighter, she worked the overnight shift in the convenience store from midnight to 8:00 a.m. five days a week, went home to care for her daughter throughout the day, and grabbed a couple hours of sleep in the afternoon before attending night classes each evening to obtain her GED. Once she had accomplished her educational goal, she decided to enroll in a community college.

Although the routine was exhausting she endured, knowing if she could earn a degree her company would promote her and she could pull herself and her child out of poverty. No hand-outs for her, unlike so many of her friends who lived off government assistance and were already pregnant again with other children.

Sophia was committed to making it on her own, and she did. Some three years after beginning her quest she gained her GED, earned her Associates Degree in Business, and was promoted to Store Manager. Within a couple of years, she would move into the corporate offices where this bilingual young executive would serve in numerous management positions, moving up the corporate ladder and becoming an inspiration to everyone she met.

The last time I saw Sophia, she was smartly attired in a gray business suit and driving her daughter to a private Catholic school in the area. She still lived not far from her own mother, which has always intrigued me since obviously they were worlds apart.

I can't help but smile when I think of Sophia and her determination to build a better life for herself and her daughter. Now that's an Oak Cliff story worth remembering.

I just wish I could recall more stories like that.

Innocence

"Out of the mouths of babes." Well, you know the rest of the saying, but recently I experienced a "gem" that was a little tarnished.

My disturbing encounter was with a two-year-old. Now I am familiar with the antics of a toddler struggling to learn the language, as I have my own bundle of atomic energy at home. My olive-skinned dark-haired beautiful brown-eyed daughter (I don't sound like a proud papa, do I?) reminds me constantly that she is two years old and proud of it.

But my conversation came not with the love of my life, but with another olive-skinned, dark-haired, beautiful brown-eyed girl of the wise old age of two. I knew that she was two, because she held up her hand so I could count her fingers and verify her age for myself.

This bright and energetic young lass and I met in her father's squalid apartment when my partner and I were dispatched to a family disturbance call. This was not a mama-papa fight, but instead one in which a mother was trying to retrieve her misguided 15-year-young daughter. The daughter had left home to live with her brother and help him raise his 2- and 4-year-old girls. The conditions of their existence in the tiny, dirty apartment were deplorable, with no air conditioning, and mats for beds.

The 15-year-old had her heart in the right place. I could see she was trying to clean the apartment to make life a little more

91

bearable for her nieces. I am sure that the father was doing the best he could, but this was one family that seemed to have the deck stacked against them.

As I walked through the compact apartment I felt a slap on my leg. When I looked down I was amazed to see this precious 2-year-old, attired in only a diaper, giving me the evil eye. I was even more astounded when I heard the toddler exclaim in no uncertain terms. "Get out of my house!" I froze in my tracks and stood flabbergasted as I listened to her continue her warning, "and don't steal anything."

I was stunned. I knelt down next to this wonderful child and showed her my badge. I told her I was a policeman and I was there to help her. Now she looked puzzled, but she held firm to her words and said "but everyone steals from us." Now let me remind you that I am in this tragic situation talking to a 2-year-old who hit me and commanded me not to steal anything. My heart sank.

This poor little girl who probably has never heard of Mickey Mouse is instead learning the cold hard facts of life on the streets. What made me feel even worse was that my mind flashed to my own daughter who looked strikingly similar, and I knew she was probably at home naively playing with her scores of baby dolls, dressing them up and taking them in her stroller to a make-believe picnic in the living room.

I did not know how to respond to this situation, so in desperation I handed the girl a card with a Dallas Police badge on it. Suddenly she seemed transformed by this token gift. She smiled and became my friend. She ran outside and showed it to all of her little cousins and held onto it like it was a diamond. Her anger and fear had been subdued, and she looked like a 2-year-old again, instead of the guardian of all that the family owned.

As I left that day, she waved goodbye to me through the window. I promised I would return to check on her and maybe, just maybe, she will remember that despite what she has experienced in life so far, not everyone will come into her house to steal from her.

The Flower

Hope. Hope for the future. Recently I had an enlightening experience, the type that every officer occasionally needs to chip away the coat of cynical armor we wear to protect and defend ourselves.

My faithful and loyal readers are familiar with kind words and beautiful sunsets that have affected me over the years, and yet this act probably was one of the most touching I have ever experienced as a public servant.

Not long ago, a disturbance call blared over the police radio, and instinctively my partner and I headed in that direction. Within seconds, the disturbance—like so many others in this increasingly-violent society—became a shooting, and by the time we arrived with lights and sirens, the shooting was a homicide.

It was a brutal crime that left a mother of three dead with a single gunshot wound to the face. To make this absurd crime even more horrifying and repulsive, the woman was killed in her own bedroom right in front of her 12-year-old son.

With parents, grandparents, cousins and friends all in the house during this early morning murder, it was absolute hysteria when we arrived.

Like most crime scenes of this nature, we would be tied up for hours as a cadre of detectives, officers, media and family all had to be tended to in one way or another. There was evidence that had to be protected, witnesses who had to be interviewed, and suspect information be gathered, just for starters. Major crime scenes always are emotionally draining, especially for the initial officers and supervisors in charge.

After about an hour and a half, another officer and I ventured outside for a walk through the neighborhood to look for some missing evidence. It was during this stroll, with thoughts of murder and mayhem on my mind, that two small children caught my peripheral vision. The innocent 2-year-old and her sister were standing behind a miniature bush silently staring at the imposing blue uniform and shiny badge. Too shy to speak, they both smiled at this emotionally-exhausted officer, and then they disappeared into the back yard.

Without much thought or feeling, I buried my nose in the ground again and returned to my narrowly-focused search of some tall weeds. After a few minutes, a pair of shadows hovering above me caught my attention. As my eyes shifted from the earth, I saw right in front of me the well-worn dresses of the two beautiful smiling barefoot Hispanic girls.

Not uttering a sound, they reached out their hands and each gave me a flower they had picked out of the yard. This gesture of friendship in the middle of a morning of murder impacted like an arrow strike to the heart, weakening my knees and bringing a tear to my eye, the kind of reaction that never shows but is felt throughout one's entire being.

These two special young children never spoke a word, simply smiled and turned away. I may never know their names, but I will never forget their gift.

The Gift

The holiday season was in full swing that year when a young woman stopped me on the street and asked where she could donate some gifts to the annual Santa Cops campaign. I thanked her for her generous offer, and promptly volunteered to hand deliver them to the Santa Cops volunteers diligently working in the property room where all of the donations are inventoried and prepared for Christmas delivery to those in need throughout the city.

She said she did not have them with her, but that I could stop by her home later in the day and gather some goodies for those less fortunate. I scribbled down her address on a piece of paper and told her that with a little luck and a light call load, I would be by in a few hours.

When I arrived after dark, her home was hardly what I expected. I realize it is not appropriate to make presumptions about people, but when this delightful young woman made such a benevolent offer, I just assumed she was blessed with money and that her home would be a palace exuding Christmas glow.

To my chagrin, this was not a high-dollar home with hand-embroidered stockings hanging from a shiny wood mantle over a huge brick fireplace. It did not have an ornament-laden tree with neatly labeled and professionally wrapped packages piled so high that the entire base of the tree was obscured with material possessions of love.

There were no life sized wooden cut-outs of Santa Claus with his diligent band of elves or his flight-ready team of reindeer. Also missing from the picturesque Christmas scene was a roof line of sparkling Christmas lights twinkling magically to the sounds of the season.

This humble home was quite devoid of most of the holiday paraphernalia we normally associate with the season's festivities. Instead, the donor of these Santa Cops toys lived in a small wooden frame house in the heart of Oak Cliff. As I entered through the front door which hung so awkwardly in its frame that gusts of wind pierced like so many frozen sabers, a cold chill ran up my spine.

Although the house was crystal clean, one could see that years of neglect had taken its toll on the scratched wooden floors, sagging ceiling, and plaster-patched walls of this low-income rental property. With old stockings hung over a portable gas heater which served as both a Christmas hearth and a source of heat, I would have expected to be delivering gifts to this house instead of picking them up.

Standing there and visually inspecting the house, I began feeling sorry for the young woman. My heart sank even deeper when I spied two small children not older than two and four years old enter the room, faces filled with apprehension and curiosity, to see what this strange man in a blue uniform and a shiny badge was doing in their home.

My eyes scanned the room in search of the answers to the questions now spinning ever more rapidly in my head. After witnessing more than my share of people begging for handouts and items they did not need, and displaying more than their fair share of greed, here were three people who were giving away a large portion of what little they had.

As my mind raced toward the end of this unfolding story, my senses brought me back to the house with its smell of hot chocolate drifting from the stove, the sight of crayon-colored pictures with handmade gifts taped to the walls, and hanging from the tiny branches of an abnormally thin Christmas tree, the sounds of two small jingle bells which announced the coming of Christmas each time the cold December air rushed through the front door.

Just as I was about to explain to the young woman and her children why I could not possibly accept the gifts (in view of the Spartan surroundings), the mother explained that she had received many gifts from agencies in the past and felt that she and her children had an excess this year. She went on to tell me that the Christmas spirit was very important to this close-knit family, and she wanted to perform a similar act of generosity for others.

Her sincerity was overwhelming, forcing me to choke back tears as the children extended their arms with the gifts they had prepared for me to take. I had no choice but to fulfill their wishes and in doing so, fulfill the wishes of others, not in the least of which was me, as I had an opportunity to view the real meaning of Christmas.

Gangs

Gangs have been a plague on our society for decades, but in Dallas during the late 1980s and throughout the 1990s gangs wreaked havoc on inner-city residents. Nightly shootings became commonplace, murders skyrocketed, rapes associated with gang initiations were a regular occurrence, and car thefts were a dime a dozen. So many cars were stolen even the gang bangers didn't know what to do with them, and it became almost a game for the young gang members to steal a car, quickly strip it, and then leave it for the cops to find so they could tow it away and the misfit criminals could steal another one.

During my years on the street, gangs were out of control, and their tentacles reached into the schools, bringing guns and drugs into the classrooms and recruiting new members to build their strength and replace those lost in shootings and arrested by police. If young adults resisted recruitment efforts, they were often ostracized by others and beaten until they finally acquiesced.

This section of Police Perspective provides a glimpse into gang life and death on the streets of the inner city.

Gangbangers

The sweltering heat of August made working the evening shift in Oak Cliff as agonizing at 10:00 p.m. as it was at noon, if not worse. The temperature was still in the 90's and without a hint of a breeze in the air. Wearing my dark blue uniform laden with all of its leather and steel accoutrements made me miserable. I could not wait for my shift to end as I turned the air conditioner on full blast in my Chevrolet Caprice squad car.

"One more hour," I thought, anxious to relieve myself of the uniform. My mind drifted to the cold beer that was waiting for me at home, as I traversed the north Oak Cliff streets of Lancaster, Ewing, and Marsalis. Since I had recently transferred to Southwest Division, I was not very familiar with the area, but I had been briefed that this particular corner of Oak Cliff proliferated with gangs. I had been told to stay alert when in the area, one of the deadliest sections of the city of Dallas.

This was the inner city, full of broken homes and broken dreams, a place where those at the bottom of the social ladder began their climb or concluded their journey. Run-down apartments operated by absentee landlords were occupied by a huge population of poverty-stricken legal and illegal immigrants from Mexico, most expecting to find the American dream, but living a nightmare. Many of the structures in that part of town had poor electricity and plumbing, and all but a few were adorned with the bright paintings or markings of gangs who controlled the neighborhood like an occupational force of troops.

Now, with only 30 minutes left in my shift, it was time to head south toward the station and the freedom of being off duty.

But that was simply not to be. I heard the dispatcher signal a major call in progress with her electronic tone alert. Instantly I spun my blue and white cruiser around as she said *"Code 3 on the shooting, 800 N. Marsalis, suspects are several Latin males about 15 years old. They are armed and on the ground in the area. Ambulance is en route, advise on a supervisor."*

I was less than three blocks away. By the time I turned on my lights and siren, I could see the crowd gathering in the street immediately in front of me. Within seconds, the area was awash in a sea of flashing lights, and only the sirens could drown out the cries and screams of pain from the frightened and shocked witnesses to this latest shooting. One look at the teenage victim, and I knew that the paramedics on the responding ambulance would only be going through the motions, putting on a good show for the family members. This young adult was probably dead before he hit the ground, since half of his skull had been removed by the large-caliber bullet.

As officers scurried to collect evidence, look for additional weapons in the crowd, and search for the suspects, I gathered the basic information on the shooting. Everyone in the crowd seemed to know who the murderer was: a young man who lived down the street, a member of a rival gang, which of course meant that the crowd was more than willing to provide me with his name, address and description, which I passed on to other officers at the scene.

In an unusual turn of events, all the witnesses told nearly the same story. In a mixture of broken English and street Spanish, they described how the shooter and some other vatos [low-rider] gang members had been waiting down the street for the victim and his friend to come home. When the victim stepped off the bus and made his way toward the apartment, he was jumped by several Los Home Boys who started shouting at him and threatening him. The victim reacted as most young gangsters in this rough neighborhood would, pulling a gun from his waistband. But before he could fire a round he was gunned down, a single shot to the head from less than five feet away. The brilliant flash of the muzzle blast cutting through the dark night was probably the last thing he saw.

Even before the crime scene investigators had a chance to process the scene for evidence, the constant chatter of the radio was broken by an officer saying that he had located the suspect hiding in a nearby apartment. Armed with a good description of the bad guy, I met the other officers and we gained entry to the apartment where we located the gunman — or, more appropriately — gun boy, as this youngster was all of 14 years old. As he and his fellow gang members were well aware, his age made him almost immune to prosecution in our abysmal juvenile justice system.

We could tell that he had been coached in what to say by members of his gang family, because the first words out of his mouth were "He had a gun and tried to shoot me, so I defended myself."

The kid was smart and knew that when all was said and done, he would get away with murder.

Split Second

During that time in my career south of the Trinity River, Oak Cliff was the epicenter of Hispanic gang activity. Burglaries, robberies, car thefts, home invasion robberies, and murders were the offenses of the day in what seemed a never-ending battle between the young gangsters and the police.

Throughout the years I have arrested countless juveniles for attempting to buy guns, or for carrying weapons in the heart of the city, where on any given day thousands of firearms are displayed by local gun and pawnshop owners. So when one of Jefferson Boulevard's conscientious and intelligent store owners called the Jefferson Storefront (my local office outside of the police substation) to tip us off to several young adults wandering in and out of stores with at least one gun, we knew this businessman was on the level. This was the same gentleman who had helped us arrest others for illegally carrying weapons, as well as assisting the police in corralling a fleeing shoplifter from an adjoining store and helping with the in-progress arrest of a burglar, all within the previous year.

Immediately after receiving the information, my partner and I took to the streets in search of five youths wearing those popular pro football jackets and armed with at least one deadly weapon. It took only seconds to spot this roving gang of juveniles as they moved eastward along the boulevard, being loud and raucous as they walked in and out of stores, disturbing the owners and clientele wherever they travelled. As we started to cross the street to get a better view, I noticed one of the young guns in the middle of the group with his coat open and the handle of a semi-automatic handgun tucked in the waistband of his trousers.

"You see him?" I asked my partner. "The one in the blue and white coat has the gun tucked in the front of his pants," I said, as we cautiously made our way across the street toward the group of young men.

As we neared the pack of juveniles, my mind became clear and sharp as I focused in on the boy and his weapon. In law enforcement, we refer to this phenomenon as "tunnel vision," as your brain automatically focuses on the most immediate danger while blocking out everything else around you. This is not necessarily good, but when it happens, one's partner becomes crucial, because with two pairs of eyes a much clearer picture of all surrounding dangers can be assessed and handled.

I do not distinctly remember at what point I pulled my 9mm semi-automatic pistol from my holster or when I assumed my familiar police shooting stance, but I clearly recall the suspect reaching for his gun in what appeared to be slow motion. The entire world seemed to slow down to where a one-hundredth of a second seemed like a minute in time.

I shouted, "Drop the gun!" as he pulled his weapon from his waistband, raised it to chest level, and pointed it at me.

I was standing in front of him now, looking down the barrel of his weapon just as he must have been looking down the barrel of mine. I started to squeeze the trigger, well aware I could be killed at any moment.

Just then I saw the fingers of his right hand open ever so slightly as his gun fell to the ground and he shouted, "It's only a toy!"

As I heard the plastic sound of the authentic-looking but fake weapon striking the concrete sidewalk, and the juvenile laughter of his friends at the big joke, I became incensed.

They were out just trying to get a reaction out of store owners and shoppers. Ages 13 to 16, three of them had already been arrested previously for the unlawful carrying of weapons. It was all a game to them, a game in which one-hundredth of a second on a four-pound trigger pull and everyone would have lost.

Close Call

Years before my encounter on Jefferson—where less than a pound more of trigger pressure would have changed my life forever—I had an eerily similar encounter that would leave an even greater impression on my psyche.

While working the evening shift, my partner and I were running license plates as we drove through various parking lots in Oak Cliff, just the sort of thing you do to keep busy or amuse yourself. Maybe you'll even get lucky and find a stolen vehicle that you can recover, kill an hour or so of the shift, and get a mark on your activity for the day. As we drove through one parking lot we noticed a vehicle parked in the back corner, facing out with its lights off. That wasn't really unusual for this restaurant at this time of evening, as many of the employees did not drive and had relatives or friends pick them up after work to drive them home.

As we cruised the parking lot, we typed in the license plate number. Within seconds a "hit" (as it's known in police lingo) came back, and the dispatcher asked our location. We advised that we were in the parking lot of a popular restaurant just down from Davis and Zang. She advised us that the car was not stolen, but did have outstanding felony warrants on the registered owner of the vehicle, thus giving us probable cause to stop and question the driver. She added that help was coming, and told us to use caution on the traffic stop.

Acknowledging the information, we decided to drive around the building and down an adjacent alleyway and approach the suspect from behind as soon as our cover was close. In a matter of seconds our backup was in position, and we made our way down the alley and lit up the vehicle, turning on our overhead red and blue lights.

My partner and I exited our car and cautiously strode toward the suspect vehicle, when the driver's previously idling engine suddenly burst into action and the chase was on. It's not unusual for related hits to come back on a vehicle even after it has been sold, but this apparently was not the case here. The bad guy thrust his car into gear, exiting the parking lot at a high rate of speed, blowing the nearby traffic light, and almost causing a major wreck before we even made it back to our squad car.

With our vehicle and another squad who had come by to cover us now in pursuit and others on the way, I was confident that this bad guy was just prolonging the inevitable by taking us on an adrenaline-filled high-speed jaunt around the neighborhood.

Up and down the streets of Oak Cliff, his car led this evening parade of lights and sounds. Unlike most chases, this driver did not feel the need to drive on major streets or head for the highway and a chance out of town. He just kept rolling around Beckley, Marsalis, Zang, and Bishop, using the side streets and cutoffs like a veteran officer.

"Get ready to run," I told my partner.

"What are you talking about? We're in a chase!"

"Not for long!" I said. "He's driving the same streets and taking shortcuts like he's lived here all of his life, which means he probably has. Also he keeps going back down the same streets over and over. He is just waiting for us to slow up a bit or make a wide turn to give him time to bail."

No sooner than the words were out of my mouth when the car ahead left the roadway and headed into a yard.

"There he goes!" I yelled to my partner, who was already jumping from the not-quite-yet-stopped squad car and in hot pursuit on foot.

Across a yard and over a fence, this guy knew where he was going. By this time, at least six officers were on the ground making their way through shrubs and around dark corners. Finally, the suspect popped out of the darkness near where he left the car and ran into the front door of a house. My partner and I both spotted him at the same time and headed for the door. Instinctively, my partner prepared to kick the door as I rushed by him, simply throwing it open and bursting into the room, yelling PO-LICE, PO-LICE—and making a mental note to tell my partner to stop watching those stupid cop shows on television where they don't even check to see if a door is open before kicking it in.

The house was filled with cops as we moved down hallways and into rooms.

"The house isn't that big, where the hell is he?" someone asked in a whisper.

Then, a noise from a bedroom, and I was the first one through the door. It was a small room with a bed, disheveled sheets and a mattress that had been moved, with a closet to my left and end table on the other side of the bed to my right. Nowhere to run, nowhere to hide. The room was dark, I was holding my flashlight in my left hand and gun in my right, and could see into the partially open closet door, just a bunch of clothes in a pile. I figured he had to be under the bed and that's why it was askew from its normal position.

Funny how that works, the assumptions police officers make everyday in a split second, assumptions that could mean the difference between life and death. My mom always made me make the bed before I left for school in the morning, with the sheets and pillow in the right place and neatly organized. At night I would climb in bed to go to sleep, and when I woke up repeat the process again. I did that for years and to this day make my children do the same, so when I noticed the sheets crumpled on the bed and the mattress slightly off base from its normal position, my assumption was that the bad guy had jumped over the bed and tried to pull the covers or mattress over himself in an attempt to hide. One little wrong assumption—but how many officers have died because of a wrong assumption?

"Where's the damn light switch?" I thought to myself as I yelled, "Come out of there. Come out from under the bed or I'll blow your ******* head off!" my commanding voice once again paying off as I saw some movement in the sheets and heard the others running in my direction.

"Come out or I swear I'll. . ." and then there's a gun, I could see it clear as day even though it was dark in the room with just a smattering of light fighting through the tattered drapes illuminating the bed.

"Drop the gun or you're a dead man!" I yelled as I watched the gun swing in my direction.

My flashlight and gun were now aligned, with the light and gun sights focused firmly on the weapon in front of me. I started to pull the trigger, but something stopped me. The gun was moving towards me but not at me, it's hard to explain, my mind tried to comprehend the situation and resolve the confusion as my heart felt like it would burst from my chest at any moment. Then the gun was pointing down now towards the bed as if the exhausted bad guy no longer had the strength to pick it up.

I hesitated and started to yell again, threatening to kill the monster under the bed. I was scared to death and the whole world seemed to be in slow motion. I saw the gun still awkwardly pointing in my direction, the rustle of the covers, movement and suddenly she appeared, popping her head up from behind the bed and dropping the gun simultaneously: a two, maybe three-year-old baby, just like my little girl at home.

My finger was still on the trigger, but I couldn't let go, my eyes were fixed on her big brown eyes shining in the low glow of the room. I let go of the trigger, but don't remember it. I lowered my gun but don't remember it. I just stared at the baby who looked at all of these men in uniform converging on her small world but did not cry.

She just stood there and I just stood there.

Off to my left I could see two other officers pulling the suspect from under the pile of clothes in the closet. I heard him yell as he was tossed to the ground and cuffed. I saw an arm reach into my field of vision and grab the gun from the bed. I just stood there and stared at my baby—I mean someone's baby—who I almost shot. An innocent little girl who had been in bed sleeping until her older brother came bursting through the door, bumping into the mattress, knocking her to the ground on the other side of the bed, dropping his .38-caliber special handgun before crawling into the pile of clothes laying on the floor of the closet.

"I almost shot a baby," I said to no one as I noticed my hand was trembling. I tried to re-holster my weapon but it was useless—my hand and the gun it was holding both shook uncontrollably. I had heard about this type of reaction from other officers, but it was a first for me. I reached over with my left hand and guided the gun into my holster, snapped the snap closed and turned back to the girl.

I'm not sure she realized what was going on. She saw the strangers in her house, men in dark blue uniforms with guns, she saw her handcuffed brother being pulled from the closet floor and taken out of the room, she saw the gun she once held onto stuffed into an officer's back pocket, and she saw the cop who almost killed her shaking on the other side of the bed. Her eyes filled with fear and then with tears.

I wanted to pick her up and hold her but I could not move. I wanted to, but my thoughts flashed between my own doe-eyed little girl and her, and it left me all but incapacitated.

Another officer entered the room, knelt by the little girl and then picked her up, carrying her into the well lighted living room. Someone was already on their way to pick up the baby's mother from the restaurant where we first encountered the vehicle and its wanted occupant. I made my way outside. I needed some air.

Someone shouted a congratulatory remark to the police pursuers, after having confirmed multiple felony warrants for a range of aggravated offenses. The driver was apparently a very bad actor and would be going to jail for a significant period of time.

I don't remember anything else that happened that night, not the jail, the paperwork, or even the ride home. What I do remember is making my way to my ex-wife's house and asking her if I could see my daughter.

She obliged and I made my way past the My Little Pony toys, into her pink princess bedroom.

I lay down next to my precious gift and just held her until I stopped shaking.

Animals in Oak Cliff

No one would expect an inner city beat cop to have an anthology of animal stories, and yet for some reason animals have always been attracted to me. When I visit the homes of friends their pets seem to gravitate to me while leaving my wife, who loves animals, alone as she scratches her head and wonders if it's my cologne. At our ranch my neighbor's donkey refuses to take food from anyone's hand but mine, and when she sees my truck pull up to the front gate her baying for my attention can be heard across the pasture.

Like any big city we have our share of rats and roaches, but it never ceases to amaze me the "pets" that inner city residents keep: from alligators to wallabys, and everything in between. I have responded to calls with guard geese who honk to warn their owners when a stranger approaches, and been pummeled by pygmy pigs when searching homes. I have seen feral cats feeding on dead bodies, illegal deer killed and hung on front porches, and cows slaughtered in backyards and barbequed for a birthday party.

Often these animals escape and find their way into the streets and onto my beat. In my work environment on the streets of Oak Cliff, this animal magnetism seemed to draw me into this series of animal misadventures . . .

Roping Horses

Driving the streets of the city each night, I meet the most interesting people in the most interesting places. Just the other evening I was diligently making my way through Winnetka Heights when, lo and behold, I stumbled upon my editor, Kathie Magers.

She was out walking her dog and getting some exercise. After a few minutes she reminded me that I had an article due for this week's paper. "I know," I said, shyly staring toward the ground because both of us knew I had not yet written it.

For some reason, Kathie reminds me of all those English teachers I had in school, and when I saw her I knew I had been busted for not doing my homework. So off I went into the Oak Cliff evening in search of a story.

What should I write about? Maybe the drug house down the street or maybe the place where those prostitutes have been hanging out for years? No, both are too-easy targets and boring material. I needed something different and exciting.

Stop a car here, make a report there, and yet the same old stories. But I was not discouraged. I have worked in Oak Cliff for too long and I know that almost anything can happen at almost any time, and usually does when you least expect it.

As my shift neared its end for the night, I still had nothing to write about. "Great," I thought, "another late night in front of the computer trying to think of something entertaining and informative."

One more stop by the 7-11--maybe Melissa and Sandy have a good story. Rats, just my luck, they already have packed it in for the evening.

And then it happened.

Just as I was about to get back into my squad car for the ride home, a taxicab comes screeching into the parking lot with its driver yelling in some almost unintelligible language (What's new about that?) that he was almost hit by two wild horses running down Zang.

"Right," I said, knowing that I did not understand a word he was saying, when another car flew into the parking lot, the driver honking and pointing down the street.

"OK, great going, John, you wanted something different and sounds like you got it," I said as I sped off in the direction that the two frightened individuals were pointing.

As I turned onto Greenbriar and made my way back up Zang, I could not believe my eyes: two huge horses were trotting down the middle of the street heading toward the 7-11. Now over the years I have done just about everything imaginable in a police car, from slow-roll processions to high-speed pursuits. Rounding up horses was not on the list, and with cars speeding around these 1200-pound-plus animals, I had to think fast.

It was obvious that the horses were not afraid of cars. I knew that the Dallas Surrey Company had stables just down the street, so I figured the pair had decided to go for a stroll without the cumbersome carriage behind them. I had to think quickly before the horses and the oncoming traffic became involved in an accident that I wanted no part of. I decided to turn on my red lights to alert the traffic, and try to scare the horses back toward their stables.

No luck. A car full of children passed by and they saw two horses with a squad car and glaring lights behind them, and a little kid in the back seat just waved. I guess he thought it was a parade.

Next plan: speed around in front of them, go against traffic, and head them in the right direction. Dangerous, yes, but seeing a huge animal go through a car's front windshield was not my idea of safety either.

Yes, it worked and the horses were heading in the right direction, back to the stables — well, not quite, because between us and their home was a beautiful patch of tall green grass. You get the picture: we stopped for their dinner.

As a matter of fact, several passersby stopped to watch two horses feeding and a cop trying to keep them out of the road.

With the backdrop of the Dallas skyline right behind us, it was quite a picture; but alas, no one was armed with a camera.

After several minutes and a call to the Dallas Sheriff's Office for some real cowboy help, Oak Cliff resident Joe Hopkins showed up. He had grown up around horses and could tell that I needed more than a little help to keep the animals safe until the Sheriff's Office showed up. In a minute, Joe was unstrapping his belt and tying it around the neck of one of the horses to keep him under control.

After some quick thinking, I sprinted over to my squad car. No extra belts, but lots of crime scene tape had to be good for something. Bingo! My ingenuity and Joe's knowledge of horses proved to be a winning combination as we fashioned halters for both animals and made a makeshift pen to keep them corralled.

Within a few minutes, a deputy from the Dallas County Sheriff's Office showed up with heavy gloves and real ropes to help us out. Of course, it took him several minutes before he could do anything, because he was laughing hysterically at the sight of this city cop holding on to two horses with nothing more than crime scene tape.

Fortunately, as soon as the deputy roped the horses, the owners crossed the bridge from the West End and took control of the horses, walking them back to the stables. What a night! What a story!

Lion's Den

I always thought it was strange that the zoo—a place for children and school trips—was located in one of the then-most crime-ridden areas of the city, until I started working there and I discovered that the menagerie was in just the perfect spot. Like many places in and around Oak Cliff, I am intimately familiar with the Dallas Zoo. I have responded to many calls there over the years, but none more memorable than a car chase that morphed into a life and death struggle and ended up as if it were a scene from a Disney movie.

It was a beautiful spring day, sun shining, breeze blowing and all was right with the world. At least that's what I thought as I aimlessly wandered the streets of Oak Cliff in my squad car. In just a few minutes I would be heading home, and with the recent time change I knew I would have more than ample opportunity to make it there and play with the kids before dinner, homework, and bedtime. As I looked forward to an impromptu baseball game with my older boys, I consciously avoided taking any calls which would result in a trip to jail and the cancellation of the backyard ballgame. I say 'consciously,' because subconsciously I was not paying attention, and I was still running license plates as I drove the streets of the city.

As luck would have it, the car travelling right in front of me was stolen. Occasionally, the officer can tell the dispatcher to "disregard," saying that he had run it earlier in the shift, but this time I had no chance because almost immediately another squad car pulled in behind me, ready for a felony stop on the stolen vehicle. My mind instantly went to the baseball game, wondering how I was going to make it home on time, when I heard the officer behind me tell the dispatcher he was in position.

"Yes!" I said to myself, because I recognized his voice and knew that he was a younger officer — which meant (according to the unwritten rules of street cops) that when the bad guy was arrested, that officer has to take him to jail. Oh, the benefits of being a senior officer! At the very most I might have to wait on the wrecker, but at this time of day the contract wrecker would be here within a few minutes and I would be on my way to play ball with my boys.

With the helicopter now notified and en route to our location, and with one car behind me and others on the way, I felt it was time to "light up" the bad guy. He knew it was coming, I had been watching his eyes in the rearview mirror. I could see him fidgeting and trying to decide if he was going to pull over and go quietly or make a run for it.

"Stay put," I thought to myself, hoping he would just pull over and it would be a quick and quiet arrest. But as usually happens, the bad guys don't like to listen or cooperate, and the chase was on.

The stolen car zoomed ahead of me and I was right on him, with my cover element behind me now calling the chase. Per department procedures, the lead car drives and focuses on the criminals, while the second car calls out the chase specifics such as the location of the chase, violations made (such as running stop signs or traffic lights) and the streets that we are coming up to, in order to assist other officers who may want to cut off the suspect or join the chase. After one works in an area for a long time you not only know the streets but have a pretty good guess on where the suspect is headed, so you can beat him to the area and make an arrest before they know where you came from.

Across Davis we headed south on Tyler Street at speeds exceeding 70 miles per hour. There were no indications that he was going to make this easy. Taking the corner on two wheels, the back of my squad car fishtailed slightly as we blew the intersection on Twelfth Street and headed east. Coming up to major intersections at Zang and the highway, I knew the chances of him making it through these heavily travelled intersections without being wrecked out were almost nonexistent, so I slowed down, expecting to see an impact.

"Where are all the cars?" I thought to myself as I made my way through the intersections and pulled back into line behind him. Across the highway, and on the service road, I figured he would head south on Ewing. This time finally I was correct, as the chase turned right alongside the Dallas Zoo. Suddenly, I saw smoke coming from the rear of his car and he veered off the road, spinning into a ditch. As his tire blew, I was right behind him.

"He's mine now!" I thought, sure that I could still make it home in time. But he bailed out of the car.

"You have got to be kidding me!" I thought as I jumped from my vehicle, now in hot pursuit on foot. This wasn't just one of our typical gangsters stealing a car for kicks or cash—he must really be hiding something, I thought, as I began the foot chase.

Down into the muddy ditch I went. I spied him running up the creek. Normally this limestone-bed creek was mostly dry and only held significant water after a heavy rain, but of course there was just enough on that day to make the foot chase even more fun, as now I was wet and muddy.

"Suspect is a black male in his late twenties; it appears he is wearing jeans and a black tee shirt with a baseball cap turned around," I yelled into the radio. I hoped my cover was still behind me in our little afternoon jog around the zoo.

I glanced up and saw large cages and laughed to myself, thinking about the time a car drove off of a nearby roadway and crashed into the monkey cage, causing a gaping hole in the zoo's security and allowing curious monkeys out to scatter throughout the local neighborhood. Talk about hysterical, watching police officers trying to track down wayward chimps and explain to citizens that they were not seeing things and yes, there were actually monkeys in their trees.

"Enough reminiscing," I scolded myself as I glanced up to see officers converging on all sides of the creek. The suspect had no way out and must have realized it, because in the blink of an eye he disappeared into a tunnel that emptied out into the creek. As I approached I could see the tunnel was pitch-black. Not knowing where it went, but assuming that it didn't just come out a few feet away, I pulled the mini-mag light from my pocket and entered it.

I could hear his footsteps. He was still running but slowing down. I yelled to him that the chase was over, he had no way out, and to come out and surrender. The suspect kept moving forward and screamed an epithet in my direction. I kept plodding ahead, not knowing where the tunnel was going to end or where I would emerge from the dark underground hole.

About fifty feet from the mouth of the tunnel I realized a few things. The first was that this was not a tunnel but a drainage pipe, which was getting increasingly smaller as I moved deeper inside the tube. My second revelation was that my radio no longer worked; I couldn't communicate to my backup and they couldn't talk to me.

I was on my own in this dark, cold pipe with a bad guy who up to this point had already stolen a car and run from the police.

The third "aha" moment was the most significant, as I felt for my gun and realized that the man I was chasing might also be armed. It was a disconcerting thought at best. I was making my way into a dark tunnel, chasing a felony suspect, who if armed might be ready and willing to use the weapon.

As I traveled further into the storm drain, it grew smaller and smaller. I was hunched over now, almost on my hands and knees, with the beam from my small flashlight being swallowed up in darkness. I could hear his breathing. He was right in front of me, but I also heard struggling and I was confused.

"What is he doing?" I thought as my light caught something now only a few feet ahead of me. He had turned around in the ever-shrinking tunnel and probably had a gun pointed right at me, not a good situation for either one of us. My mind told me that someone was going to die.

"Leave me alone or I'll shoot!" he yelled, and the sound boomed off the walls. In the tunnel, as close as we were, he could have whispered and it would have sounded loud.

"You're not going to shoot," I called, "because if you shoot then I will shoot, and we will both probably die."

Our bodies were wedged inside the tunnel with almost no room to move. Any shot in this close space would at least burst our eardrums and the bullets would pierce our bodies because there was literally nowhere else to go.

The storm drain with its steel walls now served as just an extension of the barrels of our guns. He couldn't miss. I couldn't miss. We would both be injured and probably die in that dark, cold hole in the ground. All over a stupid stolen car, for which if convicted he probably would have only been sentenced to probation. Now, we were both staring at our last moments on earth if he decided to pull the trigger.

"I'm stuck," he said.

"What?"

"I can't move, I tried to turn around to shoot you and got stuck."

"Drop your gun," I said.

"No," was the reply.

"If you are stuck the chances of you getting a good shot off at me before I shoot you 16 times [the capacity of my Sig Sauer 9mm] are very small," I made clear to my companion in the hole. "Drop your gun or die right here!"

I heard the metal weapon fall to the floor of the storm drain, echoing all of the way back toward the light. I tried to make my way towards the gun but quickly determined it was out of my reach and thankfully also out of his so I felt the situation was basically under control; that is if you believe being stuck in a drain pipe under the zoo with a fleeing felon is under control. By this time my cover was making his way down the tunnel towards me.

"Your radio doesn't work," the officer yelled.

"I know," I replied.

"Where's the suspect?"

"Right here with me" I said. "He is stuck. I need you to go back topside and find out where the access points of this drain are and call the Public Works Department to open them up and get us out of here." With that, the young officer was gone and disappeared back into the darkness.

"What do we do?" the suspect asked.

"We wait, so make yourself comfortable," I joked as our long wait began.

About twenty minutes later the young officer returned and informed me that he had good news and bad news. The good news was that the Public Works Department had located us on their map and they were en route to get us out. The bad news was that we had gone so far into the tunnel we were now located underneath the zoo. To make matters worse, as far as they could tell we were stuck somewhere in the vicinity of the lion's cage; if that was the case, they would have to clear the animals out and secure them before they could rescue us. The zoo had been notified but there was no telling how long all of this would take, so we would just have to sit and wait.

I realized that I wouldn't be home any time soon and that any chance I had for playing catch with my sons had long passed. The life of a street cop: one minute I'm driving along minding my own business and thinking about going home, the next I'm in a car chase, then a foot chase, then face to face in a tunnel with an armed bad guy. So there I was sitting inside a cold, dark pipe waiting for someone from Ringling Brothers and Barnum & Bailey to clear out the lions and lift us out of the hole.

After nearly an hour I heard commotion coming from above us. Rattling and banging, then light pouring in and voices calling to us. In short order someone descended from above and I filled him in on the situation: the suspect had dropped the gun, and if they could get him free from his wedged-in position I would make the long trek back down the tunnel.

"No need," was his response. "As long as you are right here we will just lift you out also."

I knew I was never going to hear the end of this if I was lifted out of this hole, but the pipe opening was only a couple of feet from me and it would take me a significant time to make my way back down the tunnel. I watched them lift the criminal from the hole and within minutes (against my better judgment) I was right behind him. Two younger officers already had the bad guy in cuffs and were escorting him away. Several curious onlookers were applauding as I stood up straight, stretching my bent back and futilely trying to wipe the grime from my uniform.

As my eyes adjusted to the light I could see some of the public works and zoo employees, and I thanked them for their assistance as I tried to gain my bearings to head out and search for my squad car and ride home.

"Out that way, towards the main entrance and make a left alongside the front of the zoo and it will wind back around to the creek, storm drain, and eventually your car," said a fresh faced rookie who I did not recognize. "I used to work here as a guide while I was in school," he continued sheepishly as his Field Training Officer looked on.

"Thanks," I replied.

As I moved off in the general direction he had pointed out, from behind me came a loud "ROAR." I had been waiting for that ever since I came up out of the hole. I just kept walking, knowing that over the days and weeks to come I would be hearing many more of the lion calls from my co-workers. I wondered if my sons were going to believe me when I told them I didn't make it home to play catch because I was stuck in a tunnel with a car thief underneath the lion's cage at the zoo.

I decided to tell them my car broke down. Maybe they could believe that.

Oak Cliff Python

I spent some time surfing the Internet the other day and discovered a significant amount of information. I learned about planes, trains, and animals. In particular, I was fascinated to find out that pythons are indigenous to India, Africa and Australia. For the layman, 'indigenous' means 'native' or 'living in their natural place.'

This absolutely astonished me because just last week one of our patrol officers was advised by Animal Control that a python's natural habitat was near the intersection of Davis and Montclair in north Oak Cliff.

As I recall, some concerned citizens (my sister-in-law Joanna and her friend Erika) were driving down Montclair on the way home when, to their dismay, they spotted a huge snake in the middle of the road. Not wanting to get out and personally observe this animal which appeared to be about the length of their car, they did the next best thing: they spotted one of Dallas' finest and flagged the police officer down.

Being advised that this huge dark-looking snake was slithering across the middle of the road, the officer knew immediately that he either had to check this story out or call a DWI squad.

Now, like most of us in blue, the on-scene officer never professed to being a snake expert, but upon seeing this creature, it did not take him long to realize that, 1) he was not getting close to it, and 2) he needed to call for some help!

Using a couple of squad cars, our heroes cornered the snake as best they could so it would not slither into the neighborhood. It was late, but the officers figured that pets and small children might still be about, and it would not be a good situation with this monster snake stalking the area.

Good call by the officers, because (as I also discovered during my Internet search) pythons are not venomous, but they do grow up to about 25 feet in length, and they crush their prey to death with their powerful muscles.

With the snake fairly contained, the next step was to contact Animal Control and get the snake "out of Dodge"—or at least out of the neighborhood. It was at this point that Animal Control advised the patrol officers that they could not come out because the animal was in its "natural habitat."

Yes, that's right! The intersection of Davis and Montclair is a python's natural habitat. Now I know that Animal Control is not hooked up to the Internet in their office, but c'mon, guys. . .

Briefed with this new tidbit of information—that the python was in its natural habitat and that Animal Control would not respond—the officers realized they were on their own, and no way were they going to be responsible if someone's child turned up missing. They had to do something.

After a few minutes of debate, Southwest Division's Senior Cpl. Larry Adamson was called. Larry has been around here for over 30 years, and everybody knows that when you don't know what to do, you call Larry. Also, he's not afraid of snakes, having just proved his bravery a couple of months earlier when he grabbed a snake which had coiled itself around some gas pumps and threw it back out into the field from where it came.

Now, even Larry could not throw this creature back to Asia or Africa, but he did find someone who said they would care for it and keep it as a pet. So, with a little help, Larry loaded up the snake, solved the problem, and saved the day.

Now I guess the only thing left to do is get back on the Internet and add Oak Cliff, Texas to the list of indigenous places where pythons can be found.

Cat's Meow

Working in north Oak Cliff and responding to violence from shootings to rapes, I became intimately familiar with Methodist Hospital, one of the major hospitals in Dallas and one of the best trauma centers in the city. Long before the police department staffed officers at the hospital or before Methodist had its own police force, street officers had to respond to the hospital to take calls and make reports of violence which had occurred at various locations throughout the area.

On one evening I responded to a shooting call. Upon entering the emergency room, I saw a man named Timothy with multiple lacerations to his face, from what I was told by the attending physician was a bullet. Asking what had happened, Timothy just muttered, "Stupid cat," at which point I settled myself into a nearby chair, because I knew this was going to be a story I just had to hear.

Supposedly, Timothy was having a small feud with one of his neighbors over the neighbor's cat. The cat, a fat tomcat of some type, seemed to enjoying scaling the shared fence and using this man's yard as his own personal litter box. Timothy apparently had talked to his neighbor, but it was to no avail, because the cat's owner didn't think there was anything he could do to stop the tom from crossing over and defecating in Timothy's yard.

Timothy grew frustrated and called Animal Control, only to be told they would respond, but that if the cat was not in the yard at the time they arrived Animal Control Officers would have their hands tied and could not approach the neighbor or enter into the dispute. Timothy called the police, his city councilman, and everyone he could think of to try to resolve his cat conundrum; the response from everyone was the same: there's nothing we can do—but good luck.

After weeks of cleaning up cat scat, making frustrating phone calls to public officials, and conversations with his neighbor that went nowhere, Timothy decided it was time to take matters into his own hands. He secured a slingshot and decided to step the battle over the not-toilet-trained tabby up a notch. He figured kids use these things all of the time, so how difficult can it be? With that, Timothy practiced in his back yard with stones and small pebbles until he felt he was a reasonably good shot.

Now he was prepared: all he would have to do is sit and wait. Wait he did, for hours on end, until the cat finally appeared for his evening constitutional. With slingshot in hand and an ample supply of pebbles, the man lined up his shot and fired. The pebble flew through the air but dropped short of its intended target. Not one to be dissuaded by a small failure, Timothy quickly loaded another rock into his weapon, took aim, and fired away, this time adding an extra little oomph to his shot. The rock went airborne, struck the fat cat in the side, and bounced harmlessly off, with barely a nod from the feline. As if in a display of one-upmanship, the cat wagged his tail in the direction of its pursuer and then casually strolled back up and over the fence.

Timothy was furious; the cat had all but spat in his face after he pooped in his pansies. This battle over Tim's turf would have to be taken to a new level in the morning, as Timothy had decided it was time to buy a gun. Timothy knew he could not legally own a gun; he was a convicted felon currently on probation. The risk of getting caught with a gun and going back to jail — especially over a stupid cat — was just too great. So in order to avoid any legal wrangles he decided that a BB gun was his best option. It was small and easy to handle but with the firepower he felt he needed to take down the tabby.

The next day Timothy drove to his nearest big box retailer and purchased his weapon: a Daisy BB gun with fixed sights, along with enough BBs to last him into the next millennium should he ever have to handle another cat caper again.

All day long Timothy practiced with his new firepower. He even drew a picture of a cat on a piece of cardboard, cut it out and placed it in the exact location where the cat had been doing its dirty act in his yard. After several hours of bull's-eye perfection, Timothy felt he was ready, and took up his position out of sight.

Patiently Timothy waited with gun in hand until he saw his intended target scale the fence and make his way into the yard.

"Wait, wait, wait," he thought, "let him get closer, I've got him in my sights," and then he blasted away. The small projectile flew out of the barrel and made its way straight for the cat; in a moment he would hear the cat's cries and then see it scurry over the fence and never be seen again.

But alas, our great hunter was not to secure his trophy that day. Just as before, Timothy had struck the cat squarely in its side, but the tabby barely flinched. The pellet from the Daisy BB gun was simply not powerful enough. Timothy had practiced all day and could watch as the tiny bullet travelled its arching path towards the target, but how was he supposed to know about BB guns? Now that his latest tactic had failed, what was he to do?

For days Timothy pondered this question, growing more frustrated and angry by the moment. He really didn't want to purchase a gun and risk going back to jail. As a matter of fact, he really didn't want to kill the cat, he simply wanted to scare it enough that it would never come into his backyard ever again. After about three days he had decided on the solution.

He needed more firepower, but since he could not legally purchase a gun, he decided that the next best thing was to get a bullet. Not a gun but what if he just secured a bullet? He was sure he could figure out a way to basically launch it at the cat without using a gun.

A little more thought and Timothy had figured out that a gun was simply a device that has a firing pin which strikes the center of the bullet, causing the primer to ignite and the projectile to be shot out of the casing. If he could replicate the scenario, he could shoot that terrorizing cat without ever purchasing a gun. So with a little work Timothy slipped his lone bullet into a vise, found a nail about the size of the primer on the bullet, and armed himself with a hammer.

Now he was ready and the waiting game began again. He had the cat's routine down now and he didn't have to wait long before the cat scaled the fence and crawled into the yard to do its business. Timothy held the nail in his hand, adjusted the vise so the bullet was pointing right at the cat, swung the hammer back, and struck the nail.

To say that Timothy had not really thought out this scenario is an understatement. As any gun owner will tell you, the purpose of the firing pin is to strike the primer of the bullet, causing an explosion of gunpowder and release of the projectile. What Timothy did not include in his formula was the purpose of the barrel: to direct the bullet out of the barrel and towards the target.

As soon as he struck the nail with the hammer, the shell casing exploded in a dozen different unpredictable and uncontrollable directions. The blast caused multiple lacerations on his face and neck and embedded numerous metal shards into his skin, sending him to the hospital for medical attention.

At the conclusion of his narrative, Timothy asked if I was going to take him to jail.

I asked him if he hit the cat.

"No," he responded, "he just jumped back over the fence."

"Well, since you didn't hit the cat I guess that can't be considered animal cruelty and because you did not possess a gun you technically didn't violate your probation, so no, you're not going to jail," I said, making my way to the door and exiting the hospital with a Cheshire-sized grin on my face.

A few days later I stopped by Timothy's house to check on the situation. He was a man possessed with getting rid of the cat, and my sixth sense told me he was not going to let himself be beaten by the animal. He had bought a slingshot, BB gun and built his own firing device, so I just knew he was going to buy something else to solve his problem.

I parked in front of the house and made my way around the side to the back gate to peer inside. Sure enough, just as I suspected, Timothy had purchased something to solve his problem.

Right there in the middle of the yard where the terrible Tom had been defecating was a yellow litter box.

Dead Wrong

As I have learned over the years, not all animal stories have a happy ending. Remember the tale of Old Yeller? I don't think he fared too well. On the streets, most of the dog tales are equally as tear-jerking. Mangy animals that are not cared for roam the inner city streets like a pack of wolves searching for whatever scraps they can find.

But sometimes even when the dogs are well-cared for pets, the stories don't have a happy ending. Such as the time I responded to a call from one pet owner regarding a young boy terrorizing his animal.

The man called the police to complain that every day, a pre-teen taking his usual path home from school would pick up a stick and run it along the fence where his pit bull was being kept. The noise of the stick rattling the fence drove the dog crazy and he would run, bark, and charge at the fence, causing quite a commotion up and down the street.

The dog owner said that he had warned the boy on multiple occasions not to terrorize his dog, but the youngster didn't seem to care. The man was searching for answers, and I made a few suggestions such as keeping the dog inside or out back during the hours immediately following school. I said I would keep a lookout for the boy, and if I saw him I would issue a stern warning and maybe scare some sense into him.

As luck would have it, the next few days were extremely busy and I did not have an opportunity to search for the lad after school. That may have been unfortunate for everyone involved, as three days later I responded to yet another call at the same address. This time it was a shooting call. With multiple scenarios playing out in my head as I sped to the scene, I wondered what had happened. Did the dog owner shoot the boy? Did he shoot his own dog? Did someone else shoot the dog, or was this just a coincidence?

As I approached the house I could see an ambulance and fire truck already at the address. I pulled in behind them and jumped into the back asking the paramedics for the scoop.

"What happened?"

"You mean this time, or last time we were here?" was the response from one of the firemen. Another was currently pushing IV fluids and applying pressure to a gunshot wound to the chest. Chaos—a man about to die right in front of me—and I knew there was a story behind it.

The fireman told me this was the second time in less than two hours they had responded to this address. The earlier call involved an 11-year-old-boy who had been mauled by a pit bull.

Apparently, the kid was banging on the fence, tormenting the dog, and the gate had been left open or unsecured. How ever it played out, the dog savagely attacked the boy, causing massive injuries, and what the firefighter guessed would be many months of surgeries and rehabilitation.

The man before me on the gurney (with an oxygen mask obscuring his face and blood from a gunshot wound spread across his chest) was the dog's owner, the very man who had called a few days before asking for help. Apparently, after the pit bull attack on the young man, the boy's father had returned to this house to extract his own form of justice on the dog owner by shooting him in the chest.

Now we had a kid nearly mauled to death and a dog owner gasping for his last breaths.

I started to take down the information for my report but there was no time to waste, the ambulance had to get the dog owner to the hospital before he died. I followed the ambulance as it sped along the streets in its attempt to save another life. As my mind swirled with questions of how this could have happened, another shooting call crackled over the police radio. This time it was a shooting at the hospital, the very location we were heading. Other officers checked "en route."

Even though it was only a little past five in the evening, I knew this was going to be a very long night.

Pulling into the emergency room parking lot, I ran up over the curb and onto the grass because there was no more room. Ambulances, police cars, and people running everywhere.

As I watched the paramedics unload the dog owner I could also see that officers were walking someone to their squad car. They already had the suspect from the shooting in custody. I approached the officers to inquire about the latest events, and they informed me that the suspect walked into the emergency room where a boy was being treated for a dog attack, and shot the father of the mauled boy, claiming that man had shot the suspect's father.

My head was spinning. "What is the victim's condition?" I asked.

"Dead," was the response.

"And he just surrendered?" I asked.

"Yep. Shot the dad, walked outside, laid down the gun, and waited for security to come snatch him up before we got here. Said he was already a three-time loser, knew he would spend the rest of his life in prison, so why run?"

I was stunned: a little boy horribly mangled, two fathers dead, and a son going to jail for probably the rest of his life, all because of a boy who rattled a dog's cage one time too many.

Just when I thought I'd seen it all, I remembered I still had over half a shift to go that night.

The Darkest Side

It may seem like an oxymoron, but life on the streets is filled with death on the streets. From homicides to suicides and—the most traumatic for me—officers killed in the line of duty. Cops just doing their jobs protecting and serving, and in a blink of the eye entire families are destroyed. I have seen more than my fair share of both officers and citizens who have left this world way too soon.

The memories are forever etched in my mind. The teenager who bled out in my arms after being shot during a gang initiation; the baby left abandoned in the creek; and the officer whose car was ripped to shreds as he sped to help a fellow officer in need. No need for notes to refresh these memories, dreams and nightmares that I share with you here.

Maybe this cathartic action it will bring me some peace. Am I doing this for me or you? I guess you can decide.

Clean Shot

Most suicides are nasty, bloody, or just horrifying to look at. The most common—gunshot wounds to the head—often spray brain matter and skull fragments across the room to be embedded into doors, walls, or ceilings. Dead bodies are not usually attractive in any form, but suicides seem to be the worst: from hangings where the victim's eyes are bulging out, to poisoning victims frothing from the mouth.

However, one suicide that I worked had to be one of the cleanest on record. Now women traditionally commit suicide in a manner that makes the smallest mess and inconveniences those left behind the least, but this young lady took cleanliness to the extreme. Tall, blonde, in her early twenties and absolutely beautiful, it would have appeared that this young woman had everything going for her—yet sometimes those inner demons prevail.

When I pulled up behind her car, responding to a suspicious person call in the neighborhood, I did not know what to expect: maybe some burglars casing a house, a custody battle in full swing spurred on by a judge's ruling, or maybe a pair of star-crossed lovers displaying their affection for each other as they steamed the windows of their car. That's one of those intangible aspects of the job: never knowing what is around the next corner, bringing the excitement and adrenaline rush that goes with walking into the unknown and trying to survive whatever the streets throw at you.

As I approached the vehicle I could clearly see inside, and noticed only one person. My theory of star-crossed lovers went by the wayside as I tried to determine if my suspicious person call was going to be dangerous, or just another one of those "OK, I understand, but let's move along now and you can finish your conversation tomorrow morning." As beat cops, we see it all many times over, and have pre-planned speeches to fit the occasion. More than once I wished I had a tape player in my pocket so I could just push a button and the automated speech would play.

I was now standing outside and just to the rear of the driver's door. It's a scene you have watched on television a thousand times, where the officers strategically place themselves in a defensive position in order to respond to any attacks by the driver. You know the kind of stance I'm referring to: where the officer has his off-hand foot slightly ahead of his gun-side foot, and his off-hand reaching towards the driver's door as his gun hand slides back close to his holstered weapon.

This time I could see the driver was not going to be a problem. As a matter of fact, the statuesque blonde was lying back in her seat motionless as if passed out, and her hands were in plain sight. I could see her purse partially open and laying on the passenger side floorboard; no threat there either. I used my flashlight to bang on the window, with no response. I tried the door and it opened easily. I yelled for her to get up and out slowly. No response. I took a closer look at her face and realized there was not going to be a response.

Not now, not ever again.

Her hair cascaded over her shoulders and looked as if it had just been brushed. Her make-up was perfect, with no signs of mascara running from tears, and yet the grayish tint to her skin and dull lifeless eyes made it painfully obvious that this young lady was dead.

The question now was, "Why?"

I looked for signs of foul play or trauma but could see nothing out of the ordinary. I checked around the car and found nothing out of place. Here was a beautiful young girl dead, with no apparent signs of injury, let alone any evidence of foul play. Had she killed herself, or did someone else do the dirty deed and then clean her up and pose her body?

She could have committed suicide by overdose, so I searched for a pill container, needle, or crack pipe, but there was nothing to suggest any of these seemingly reasonable explanations. I leaned over the body to search the purse for prescription pills or illegal drugs, but found neither.

Reaching to the bottom of the purse, my fingers touched cold steel; I immediately suspected that this would not be a natural death. I pulled a small caliber revolver from her purse, opened the cylinder and discovered that one .22-caliber bullet had been fired. It being a revolver explained why I didn't find a shell casing on my initial cursory search of the vehicle, because the spent casing was still in the weapon.

OK, I thought, now we have a gun and one bullet fired, but at whom? Was she defending herself and fired at an assailant who had escaped after killing her? Maybe he had strangled her and posed her in that position and for whatever reason the bruises were not yet visible on her neck. There was no blood on her or in the car; if the offense had happened in the vehicle, surely there would have been blood if there was a shootout of some kind.

No blood, no entry wound, and no exit wound. This was getting interesting.

I figured that I had done all that I could do without disturbing the body. I waited for the Medical Examiner to see if we could unravel this mystery of the beautiful dead woman in the sports car in the middle of the inner city. Once the ME was on scene we were able to move the body and check for wounds, and on first examination found nothing. I just knew that there would be a small pool of blood on the seat behind her back and underneath her, but it was the cleanest crime scene I had ever seen.

I picked up the purse to show the ME where I had discovered the pistol, and pulled its contents out for a closer look. Her identification was inside; I had looked at it earlier in an attempt to identify her and make some inquiries into what had happened and maybe notification of the family.

As the ME examined the license I pulled a wad of Kleenex from the purse. It was neatly folded and appeared as if it had never been used. I was going to throw it on the seat when it started to unfold and I noticed a small amount of blood; it wasn't much, no more than a few drops, but it was definitely fresh blood. So at some point in the evening, the young woman was bleeding and had folded up the Kleenex and placed it neatly in her purse instead of just throwing it on the floorboards or out the window. This young lady didn't want to make a mess.

The picture was becoming clearer now as my mind flashed back to training from many years gone by. Most women don't use guns to commit suicide, because guns are too messy and they do not want others to have to clean up after them. Obviously this woman went more than then extra mile to leave a clean crime scene.

The ME returned to examining the body. There were no visible gunshot wounds upon first glance, but now it was time for a much closer look. The ME ran his gloved hand over head, face, neck arms and legs, to no avail. Next he ran his hand over her chest, moving her blouse and examining her bra — and there it was. On the underside of her bra was a small red spot of blood. The ME moved her bra aside and lifted her left breast, and the picture finally became clear with the appearance of the entry wound of a small caliber bullet, matching the small caliber gun in her purse. The bullet would later be found lodged in her spine, hence no exit wound, and no blood underneath or behind the victim. I asked about the lack of blood on her front and the ME surmised that the gunshot had been a close contact wound, so close that the weapon almost cauterized the wound as the bullet entered, resulting in almost no loss of blood. What little bleeding did occur was neatly cleaned up by her tissues.

Apparently this lovely young lass had decided that life was no longer worth living. She secured a .22-caliber revolver and drove from her northern suburban home to the inner city, found a secluded street, and placed the gun to her chest. She fired the weapon one time into her heart, causing a fatal wound. Somehow after pulling the trigger, she cleaned the wound, folded the tissues, and placed the tissues and weapon back in her purse on the floorboard before lying back in her seat to quietly die.

There are a host of questions I would have liked to ask her about her death, and maybe more important, inquiries about her life and what precipitated the horrendous series of events. Maybe that's what so difficult about suicides: not the actual death, because we all will die, and not even the manner of death—as street cops we witness horrific ends to life—but the questions that we never get to ask and never really find answers for.

Most suicides leave more questions than answers.

Ricochet

I vividly recall one shooting that left no one wondering, but it did leave all of us shaking our heads and saying to ourselves that familiar refrain "Just when you think you have seen it all..." Now, I know that just my having a 'favorite suicide story' speaks volumes by itself, but as a coping mechanism officers often look for and find humor in the strangest places. This story certainly qualifies.

While on patrol one night I responded to a suicide call on Fort Worth Avenue in far north Oak Cliff. When I arrived at the tiny wood-framed structure I discovered a gentleman in his mid-fifties, with scraggly beard, old blue jeans and disheveled tee shirt, and with a pair of bullet wounds to his jaw and cheek. Amazingly, he was not only alive but, except for the primarily superficial wounds, in good condition.

The paramedics worked on him for a few minutes, and told me that his injuries were non-life threatening; the gun he was using was a small-caliber rifle, and when he placed it under his chin it apparently slipped and simply shot a glancing blow off his lower jaw and out through his cheek. He would need additional medical attention, but would be fine.

After a few more minutes the man was able to talk to me, and the first thing he said was, "Now that I'm fixed up, you had better go look at her," pointing in the general direction of his kitchen.

"Her who?" I asked, making my way into the other room, where to my complete surprise I discovered the freshly dead body of a middle-aged woman.

"What happened?" I shouted towards the man as I yelled for the paramedics to come help with this latest victim.

The story he related to me would have been unbelievable if I had not been there on the scene to verify it.

The gentleman told me that he had come home from work as usual after a 12-hour day of manual labor, and that his wife began nagging him about the bills, money, house, etc. He said that he had lived with her constant nagging for years and could not take any more of it.

He told her if she didn't shut up he was just going to kill himself.

She said she didn't care, so he walked over and grabbed a .22-caliber rifle from the closet. He loaded the rifle and sat down on the couch, placing the butt of the gun on the floor between his legs with the end of the barrel underneath his chin. He thought this might finally shut her up, but her ranting and raving continued. As a matter of fact, she told him that he was "so stupid that he couldn't even kill himself the right way and that if there was ever anyone who could screw up his own suicide it would be him." The nagging became so unbearable and her tirade so hateful, said the middle-aged man, that he couldn't take any more, and he pulled the trigger.

But he was so upset and shaking so badly that the butt of the gun moved. Instead of the bullet striking him under his chin and going through his head and into his brain, killing him instantly, the bullet made a glancing blow off his jaw, exiting between his upper lip and his cheek.

"But what happened to her?" I asked, pointing at the deceased wife.

This is where the story really got crazy. The man said the pain from the shot to the face caused him to lose consciousness briefly, but he distinctly remembered hearing a ping. When he awoke he discovered he wasn't dead, just bleeding, but his wife wasn't nagging him any more. He got up from the couch to investigate, and discovered her dead in the kitchen, with a single bullet wound to the head.

Apparently, instead of penetrating the fleshy part of the man's jaw and causing a fatal injury as it made its way through his skull and into his brain, the bullet glanced off his jaw, changing its trajectory and causing it to exit his cheek, hit a water heater that was standing in the corner of the tiny home, ricocheted off the heater, then travelled approximately five feet from the living room through an open doorway into the kitchen, thereby striking his wife in the forehead and killing her instantly.

The paramedics said they could only find one small bullet entrance wound to her temple, and no exit wound. I checked the water heater, and sure enough there was a mark consistent with a bullet striking it and ricocheting off of it. Since the gun was a single-shot rifle, and there was only one spent casing in the room, it all added up.

When all was said and done, the District Attorney chose not to file on the man for any offense. You see, suicide is not illegal, probably because if you are guilty of it there is no one to prosecute because—by definition--they are dead. Attempting suicide is a minor misdemeanor, where more often than not mental health services are required.

As for an involuntary manslaughter charge, the man's story along with the evidence was so compelling—coupled with the fact that his wife was even in a different room and no one could have foreseen such an odd scenario of events playing out—that no charges were ever filed.

In the end I guess his wife was right about him being able to screw up his own suicide.

But then again, I guess he finally got her to stop nagging him.

The Tape

I still have the first book my parents ever gave me about being a police officer. It is titled *Our Friend the Policeman,* by David Cunniff. I must have been less than two years old when my mom first read it to me, and I am sure it was one of the first books I ever learned to read. To this day I can recite the book almost verbatim, especially the pages that say:

> **Painters paint pictures and Carpenters saw,**
> **Our friend the Policeman enforces the law.**

Although this phrase still rings true today, the part the author omitted for his young readers was:

> **Policemen work hard, and Policemen try,**
> **But sometimes even the best Policemen die.**

Throughout my career I have dealt with pain, suffering, and death. I would say I'm almost immune, but can one ever become totally immune to these unpleasant facts of life? I don't think so.

I can vividly remember coming into work the morning after one of our undercover officers, Larry Bromley, was killed. As soon as I walked in the door I saw it. There it was, sitting on the counter with a half dozen officers standing around it. I looked away, hoping that I was mistaken or that it might just disappear. But when I turned and raised my eyes, my heart sank. It was still there, and it was not going away.

Only the softest of whispers were audible from the men in blue who surrounded it, as if it were a wily prisoner just apprehended after an exhausting battle.

After a moment a senior officer, bearing the medals on his chest of numerous campaigns, made his way through the troops and picked up the roll of black tape. Slowly, stoically, without even a hint of outward expression, he cut off a section of tape and then returned the roll to the counter. Without a word, he placed the tape horizontally across his badge, collected his remaining gear, and hit the streets for another day of serving the community.

It was real. As real as the looks on the faces of the police officers who stood speechless in the hallway. As a lump formed in my throat, I wondered who it was for, while at the same time silently saying a prayer of gratitude that it was not for me. Then panic began to set in as I wondered again who was it for: one of my friends, a classmate, a former partner? Did I know him? Did I work with her? The questions raced through my mind as my heart pounded in anticipation of the answer.

Voices could be heard now from outside the door. It sounded like conversation and maybe even laughter, and the people in the room turned to look. As soon as the door opened, the newcomers saw it, too. Not a word had to be spoken. The jovial officers just coming to work registered shock and horror when they saw it laying on the counter. There would be no more laughter for them this day.

I made my way through the growing crowd of public servants and walked toward the counter where the tape rested. As I approached, a young officer angrily threw a newspaper down next to it. The headline was all the explanation necessary. Everyone already knew why it was there, and this confirmed our worst fears. The officer, with the fire still burning in his eyes, stormed away from the counter and out onto the streets to face another day of serving the citizens.

The lump in my throat seemed as big as a softball and the pain in my heart was simply a dull ache as I picked up the roll of tape. The words of the headline reverberated in my head as I re-read the news. Tearfully, I cut off a section of tape and reverently placed it over my badge. The beautiful blue and silver star now was broken by a band of black.

This dark symbol spoke so that we did not have to. Words were no longer necessary as we realized that a fellow officer had paid the ultimate price for serving the public.

Silently, I laid the tape back on the counter and wishfully prayed as I walked away that I would never have to see it again.

Lending a Helping Hand

One of the most emotional calls of my career occurred just as I left the station one rainy afternoon right before shift change between days and evenings. The city had been beset by a ferocious thunderstorm, one of those where the clouds continuously explode with lightning, the rain falls in sheets—sideways at times—and nearly everyone keeps an eye peeled toward the sky, watching out for the dreaded funnel cloud that signals an approaching tornado.

I had just cleared from the station and was making my way towards anywhere out of the rain. My favorite spot in weather like this was always under the protection of a car wash. In Dallas most are made of brick, providing some type of security, yet open on both ends to provide a quick escape if needed. For many officers, the car wash or underground parking structure were not dissimilar to running into a mountain cave to seek shelter from the elements.

Little did we know that on this day there would be no shelter.

As I drove west on Illinois leaving the Southwest substation the call came out, the report of a major accident on Interstate 20 and an officer down. Turning on my lights and siren and hitting the en-route button on my computer, I headed south on Loop 12 then onto southbound Spur 408, making my way through the torrential rainstorm towards the highway. Almost immediately after getting on I-20 I could see the wreck, but I was on the wrong side of the road and knew I would have to pass the accident and make a U-turn at the next exit to get around to the westbound traffic.

The officer had been doing what so many others do each and every day: just helping a citizen. In this case it was a citizen who had gotten a flat tire in the middle of the rainstorm and the officer stopped to change the tire, a selfless act of kindness that in a blink of an eye turned to tragedy.

As the young officer worked to change the tire, his vehicle was struck from the rear by another motorist who had lost control in the storm. The impact from the collision trapped the officer between the vehicles, killing him instantly.

When I arrived another senior officer was already on the scene. I could immediately tell something was very wrong as he just stood there in silence, tears rolling down his face, realizing there was nothing he could do for the young officer.

That was the first of four separate times during this one horrific incident that I almost broke down and lost it right there on the street. The first was seeing the officer down and knowing immediately that he was dead. The second time was not just because of my fallen comrade but because I knew the senior officer was a tough-as-nails type of guy, and still he had totally lost it. Years of pain and agony that had been bottled up inside now flowed down his face as readily as the rain poured around us. I silently grabbed his arm and ushered him out of the way, handing him off to some other officer and whispering, "I've got it from here."

Officers came and went, ambulances, fire trucks, supervisors and accident investigators, and through it all I stayed at the scene doing my job and trying not to break down. I had a job to do after all and could not take time out to be emotional; that was not going to help anyone.

As we were preparing to move the officer's body, I glanced off to my left where an impromptu river had formed in the median that divided the lanes of traffic on the highway. As the rain continued to pour down from the sky — as if even God was crying over this senseless tragedy — the river of water became mixed with the officer's blood which had been pooled under his body. And if this scene was not already tragic enough, the officer's hat became adrift in this ever-expanding sea of red, and I felt obligated to go and retrieve it. Wading into the red river, I grabbed the rain-soaked hat and made my way back to the ambulance to place his headgear on the stretcher.

After an hour or so I headed to my car to get something or other, or maybe just dry out a little bit. It was a trip I never should have made, because I had been so wrapped up with my duties at the scene, I failed to realize my police officer wife was also on site. When I looked up I could see her tall, lean body adorned in her yellow police rain gear, directing traffic around the accident scene, with tears streaming down her face.

How I held it together through those four trials I just don't know. But maybe even more amazing might be the fact that after hours on scene, dealing with some of the most traumatic events I've ever experienced, I simply made my way to the station, changed clothes, and went back out on the street to answer calls, help citizens and bury the entire experience deep down someplace where people can't see.

Because that's what all police officers are expected to do.

Kids

Being a father of six, I guess it is easy to understand why I have always had a soft spot in my heart for children. Mine have always meant the world to me, and if you asked my wife that's the reason we are together. When she first called me up and asked me out (that's right: she chased me), I told her I would be happy to meet her for dinner but it would have to be later, as one of my boys had a baseball game and I was not going to miss it even for a 21 year-old, beautiful, tall, blonde. As she tells it, that's when she knew I was the one. My children have always been my number one priority, and maybe that is why the calls on the street that affected me the most involved kids.

Life on the streets is difficult for even the most hardened members of our society, but for children it can be almost impossible. When born into poverty in a single-parent household with little or no guidance or direction in life, they are often consigned to a life of misery from their earliest days. Many descend into a life a crime, join a gang for some type of affiliation, or fall into the easy trap of drugs as an escape from their pain.

Here is just a small sampling of stories to illustrate what growing up on the mean streets of the inner city can be like for the most vulnerable members of our society.

Gym Class

An old police television drama used to say, "There are eight million stories in the naked city." That's probably true, and the unfortunate fact is that a significant number of those stories belong to children and young adults, individuals who are often trapped by their circumstances and, as a last resort, cry for help in the form of a 9-1-1 call. Often that call *is* their last resort.

The comments on the call sheet from the dispatcher read "Young man wants to report himself as a truant and turn himself in." My radar immediately went up: either this was a bogus call and someone was intentionally wasting the police officer's time, or it was someone trying to lure an officer into the area for some type of attack or ambush. My mind couldn't get around the comment that a kid wanted to turn himself in for being truant and thus (depending on his age) face fines, jail, or both.

In this part of the city, teenagers spent an inordinate amount of time running from the police and trying to avoid getting caught skipping school. As a matter of fact, the problem of truancy had become so rampant that a local Justice of the Peace started hauling in both kids and parents and assessing large fines for not complying with the state's compulsory attendance laws.

In law enforcement we have known for years that when kids are not in school and are out on the streets, crime increases. Idle hands lead to burglaries and thefts, and drug and alcohol abuse are always in vogue at "skip parties." So why was this young teen calling to report himself absent? I had to know the story behind the call.

As my police cruiser turned left from Eighth Street onto North Lancaster and then right onto East Seventh, I could see the dilapidated two-story brick building just ahead and to the right. This particular building was one of the many structures in the city that should have been condemned and torn down years ago. A reasonable person would not even allow animals to be kept in those conditions, yet city leaders refused to enforce city codes and tag the violations. Instead they gave in to the persuasive financial powers of absentee landlords, ridiculously justifying it by saying that demolition of these low-income housing units would leave the poor with nowhere to live. So they looked past the myriad life safety violations such as no running water, exposed electrical wires, no air conditioning in the summer or heating in the winter, and figured that somehow the poor were benefited by the city's benevolence.

This is an example of just another one of the anxieties that a beat cop has to learn to get over if you are going to remain sane and do your job. Every day, a cop sees people who are destitute and in desperate situations, and there is little or nothing you can do. You report it to the city and they tell you to be quiet and 'do your job.' You try to enforce health and safety laws, and they refuse to prosecute, saying it would set a bad precedent. Met with frustration at every turn, a cop keeps going, hoping that somewhere along the way he'll be able to help.

On this day my jaw nearly dropped when I discovered that the dispatcher was absolutely right. When I pulled up to the reported address, not only was the young man there, he was actually sitting on the front steps of his apartment building waiting for me.

"Did you call?" I asked, as I cautiously approached the young black male, who looked to be about 13 years old. He was wearing wrinkled clothes that were too small for him and which (if my nose was working correctly) had apparently not been washed in days.

"Did you call?" I repeated, and he nodded his head in the affirmative.

"What's your name?" I asked, hoping for a verbal response this time.

"Kenyon," was his reply.

"What do you want, Kenyon?" I asked, as I moved closer to the seated youngster.

"Sir, I'm not in school, so you can just take me to Juvie [Juvenile Center]."

"Did you commit a crime?"

"No."

"Then why do you want to go to Juvie?" I continued my line of questioning to this unusually-respectful young man.

"I really just want to go to school, but I thought if I told the 9-1-1 lady that, you wouldn't come."

"Good thinking," I responded," she probably would have referred you somewhere else and by the time they showed up, school would be over. Where's your mom and dad?"

"Don't have a dad. Mom's inside, she's sick and can't take me."

"She need an ambulance?" I queried.

"Not that kind of sick," he answered.

Before I could ask my next question, he spelled out the story in detail. He told me that his mom was a crackhead and a prostitute. Sometimes she would show up with tricks, trying to make the last few bucks for the night, but mostly she would hit the dope house on the way home and then stay high all day, usually passing out, and only on the rarest of occasions performing any motherly chores such as cooking or cleaning. Kenyon made sure that I understood that she was not a bad mother—she just had a problem. I nodded as I listened to this sad but all-too-common tale.

I told Kenyon he seemed to be very intelligent and mature for such a young age, knowing that in this part of town too many young people have to grow up and face the harsh realities of life all too soon. Now it was his turn to nod.

I asked him if he liked school, and he gave the typical teenage response, "It's OK."

"Then why do you want to go to school?" I asked him, still perplexed by the 9-1-1 call.

"Well, I was hoping to get there before lunch."

It was starting to make sense. "When was the last time you ate?"

"I don't know, maybe a few days ago. My mom cooks for me whenever she can, but she's been sick a lot lately."

I could tell that he used the 'sick' term about his mother on a regular basis, probably to friends, family, and even teachers. Before I could offer him a ride to school, Kenyon continued with why he wanted to go to school. I learned that it wasn't just for the free meal, but because sometimes after PE class when no one else was around, one of the coaches would let him take a shower and then gave him some used school sweatpants, tee shirt, or sweatshirt to wear. A meal, a shower and some clothes might not seem like much to most folks, but to Kenyon they were a Godsend.

"You gonna take me to Juvie?" Kenyon asked.

"No," I replied. "How about I take you to school and on the way we make a run by Jack in the Box? I don't think anyone would complain about you having two lunches, especially if they knew you missed breakfast." His eyes lit up and before I knew it he was on his feet and ready to go. Two Bonus Jacks, an order of fries, and a milkshake later we were at school, where I dropped Kenyon off at the front door. I then circled the building and went in the side entrance to visit with his counselor.

The counselor was familiar with some of Kenyon's story, but not all of it, and had assumed that when he said 'sick' he meant it in a literal way. She pledged to call Social Services and to dedicate some additional time to Kenyon's situation, all the while letting me know how overworked she was because there were so many middle-school-aged children in the same or similar situations. I also pledged to look in on him—but other than writing up a report and sending it to Social Services, I never did.

A couple of months later I did run into Kenyon's mother. I responded to a disturbance call at his apartment and found the mother drugged out of her mind, armed with a hammer and giving a thorough beating to one of her boyfriends or tricks, I couldn't really tell and didn't care.

On the way to jail I asked about Kenyon, and she told me he now lived with her sister in another part of town. She never asked how I knew him, or why I cared.

No father, a drug-addicted mother in jail, and a son shipped off to live with relatives.

Call for Help

One young adult just a few years older than Kenyon did reach out for help, and I was happy to be of at least some temporary assistance.

Stephanie was 16 years young when I responded to a 9-1-1 call from one of her girlfriends. The dispatcher relayed to me that the anonymous caller had stated during a conversation earlier in the evening that Stephanie had threatened to kill herself. Not wanting to betray her friend, yet truly concerned for her safety, the teenager sought counsel from her mom before finally deciding to call the police.

When I pulled into the upper middle-class area of Kessler Park, I knew that a suicide call was not out of the question. I had responded to several suicides in this distinguished neighborhood over the years: distraught lovers, failed businessmen, and even a friend of mine who could just not put his family through the last stages of his debilitating illness. Each of them in his own way had decided to end it all in this tree-lined bucolic neighborhood where serious crime had never gained a foothold.

It was about 6:30 in the evening when I rang the doorbell to the residence and announced my presence to the astonished mother.

"No one here called the police. We're fine, thank you," she said as she began closing the door.

My foot intervened and I said, "I need to talk to your daughter before I can leave."

Perturbed by my presence, the woman reluctantly called for Stephanie, who appeared at her bedroom door in short order.

"This officer needs to see you're OK and that we don't need the police," the mother hollered over her shoulder.

I asked the young woman, "Can I talk to you?"

"Sure," was the response as she moved slowly into the living room. Shoving my way past the unwilling doorkeeper (who was in my humble opinion wearing clothes just a little too young for her age), I explained to Stephanie why I was there. I told her we received a call from her friend who was worried, and just wanted to make sure that Stephanie was all right.

Stephanie admitted talking to her friend after school, and maybe saying something about how distraught she was at breaking up with her boyfriend before the school dance, but said that was just talk and she really didn't mean anything by it. She said she was sorry for making me come out.

The look on her face told me a different story. I asked to speak to her alone, knowing her mother would adamantly object. But just then the phone rang, and the mother decided that answering the call was a more pressing matter than her daughter's threat of suicide.

With mom now engrossed in her phone conversation (with what from her voice and behavior I could tell was a male caller), I walked with Stephanie into her bedroom. She sat on the bed and tears welled up in her eyes.

"Do you want to tell me the real story?" I asked.

"How did you know?" she replied.

"I've been doing this a long time," I said.

Stephanie began to speak, telling me that her dad had left home nearly a year ago and had hardly been in contact since. She adored her dad, he meant everything to her, and she was crushed by his leaving. She hated her mom and her lifestyle with its wide variety of boyfriends nearly every week. To make matters worse, her mom was a drug abuser, and Stephanie hated everything about her life. She just wanted to be away from her mother and back with her dad again.

Stephanie went on to say that she was terribly depressed and that her A grades in school were now tanking, along with her life. I asked her if she really had spoken to her friend about committing suicide, and she said she had. I asked her to tell me what she had said and was astonished at her answer. This beautiful young woman of barely 16 years, with her long brunette hair and a face that professional models would envy, told me that not only had she thought about committing suicide, but she knew exactly what she was going to do.

Stephanie told me that her mother had recently purchased a handgun as protection against the unruly and often-criminal men she had been entertaining at home in recent months, men who had more than once traded drugs for sex and then administered a beating because they were asked to leave the house before dawn. Stephanie's plan was to wait until her mother was asleep in bed, then to quietly sneak into the room and without making a sound, open the top drawer to the nightstand on her mom's side of the bed and grab the gun from its hiding place there. Once she had the gun, she said, she was going to kneel down right beside her mother's head. Then, placing the gun in her mouth, she would wake her mother so that the last thing her mother would see was her daughter shooting herself in the head.

I would not have believed my ears, but as I looked into the young woman's eyes I knew she was speaking the truth. Stephanie hated her mother and her mother's lifestyle, and she loved a father who was probably never coming back. Stephanie was determined to make a statement that her mother would never forget.

After I heard her story, it was a no-brainer to take Stephanie into protective custody. Not only was she severely depressed, but she had a plan and a means of carrying out her threat. She was definitely a danger to herself and needed help, and I had responded to too many suicides in this neighborhood already. With less resistance than I would have expected, her mother let me take Stephanie to Child Protective Services to get her the counseling and services she needed.

I don't know whatever became of Stephanie; as street officers, we rarely knew the outcome of such situations. But I can tell you that I never heard of another call at her residence and never saw a report of a suicide, so I could only hope that my intervention that evening stopped a suicide and saved a life.

Sheet Rock Angel

On another unforgettable call involving a juvenile, I responded to a domestic disturbance at the home of a Hispanic female.

As soon as the door swung open I knew there was going to be trouble. Not from the meek and mild older female who answered the door, but from the hysterical teenager who wanted a fight and, before the night was over, was going to get his wish.

I stepped inside as the small and frail-looking woman explained that she was okay, that she and her son had simply had an argument and that's why she called the cops. She added that the dispute was over now and we were not needed. Her story was so weak and her look so helpless that I could tell that the abuse ran much deeper; she had probably been a victim of violence for many years. I began to explain that since this was a domestic violence call we could not simply leave the offender and victim in the house together, and one of them was going to have to leave.

About that time the rebellious teenager started to mouth off to both his mother and me. Now, I've never had a high tolerance for people bad-talking their moms, and could never even imagine using such language in front of my mother, but when it comes to disrespecting an officer in uniform I quickly drew my line in the sand. I told him in no uncertain terms, "One more word out of you and you're going straight to jail, I don't care what your mother says."

Just then I heard the front door open behind me. I knew that it was my cover officer because I heard him on the radio marking out with me just moments before he came through the door. As I turned to my partner to instruct him to cuff the teenager, I noticed the strangest sight I had ever seen on a domestic violence call. There on the sheetrock wall next to the door was an almost perfect indentation of the shape of a person—a small person, more specifically, the dainty mother of the youth. I could not believe my eyes. I could see exactly where her head, torso, and butt had hit the wall. She had been thrown so hard against the wall by her son that she literally made a near full-body indentation in the sheetrock.

It was time for me to lose it. I turned to the teen, pointed in his direction, and said something like "You piece of crap – your butt is mine!" as I lunged toward him.

Now that's an old police trick, because a good officer never tips his hand. You always want to keep the other person off guard in case he wants to fight or run, which they are less likely to do if they are caught by surprise. Conversely, if you want to encourage a fight or car chase you tip your hand early, hoping that the bad guy will think that he has enough time to either get away or get in a few good punches.

Tipping one's hand was a good tactic on nights when you were bored and maybe wanted to spice up the evening by getting into a car chase. Instead of "lighting up" the violator when you were right behind him and he knew he had little or no chance of getting away from the police, you would turn on your red lights and siren a half-block or more behind the offender. For many young criminals, when they looked in the rearview mirror their bravado and/or inexperience would kick in, and before you knew it, a simple traffic stop could become a heart-pounding car chase and arrest that would break up even the most mundane shift.

On this night, however, my intention was three-fold: to signal to the teenager that he was about to go to jail, and to allow him to throw the first punch, which would add to his charges, and to warn my unsuspecting partner that the fight was on. The teen responded just as I expected, and swung wildly at my head before being knocked down by officers tackling him from two directions. Within seconds he was handcuffed and being led kicking and screaming to the back seat of the squad car.

As my partner sat with the youthful abuser, I went back inside to get more information from the victim for my report. The woman confessed that the abuse had been going on for years, and that she didn't know what to do. Before I left, the kindly woman thanked me for taking her son and helping her.

I thought the encounter with the gentle woman and her manic son was over until I received a subpoena to appear in Juvenile Court. Apparently the prosecutor had reviewed my report and sided with me on the long-running abuse, and was asking for jail time for the bad kid. The mother was refusing to press charges, but was advised that it was not her choice since this was a domestic violence case and the State could serve as both the complainant and prosecutor. Thus I was forced to go to court to testify. By the time I arrived at court, the mother had decided that the event never happened at all, and that I had made up the entire story just to arrest her poor innocent son who had never harmed a flea.

I came to the quick realization that if the Judge believed the mother, her abusive son would walk away free. I knew from experience that the beatings the son gave his mother would not only continue, but would get progressively worse. I asked the Judge if I could approach the bench and speak to him privately. He agreed and I quickly made my way to the front of the courtroom to tell him what had happened that night, and, more important, what I had observed, most notably the life-sized indentation in the wall. He was appalled, and we decided upon a course of action.

After I took my place in the courtroom, the Judge informed the mother that if she took the stand and testified that the event never happened, and that if I countered her testimony with my police report and my testimony, he would be forced not only to rule against her but to order me to immediately place her under arrest for filing a false police report and for perjury. In that case, not only would her son be sent to jail, but she would be joining him. The Judge was so adamant about his plan of action that he ordered the prosecutor to go into the hallway and find a defense attorney who could advise the mother on the appropriate course of action before she spoke again in court.

The prosecutor did as he was instructed. Within a few minutes an attorney was secured, and he approached the bench to be briefed before meeting with his new client. In less than an hour the mother, under advice from her new attorney, recanted her recanted story. She decided not only to testify against her son, but once on the stand she let go with both barrels. She described the years of abuse since the boy's father (who was also an abuser) had left, and how on one occasion her son had thrown her so hard against the wall that her body actually made a life-sized indentation in the sheetrock.

I never even had to testify. The street-wise Judge threw the book at the teenage delinquent, immediately remanding him into the custody of the Juvenile Detention officers.

I don't know how much time the young criminal received for his assault. But it was nice for once to see a domestic violence victim stand up to her offender, even though it took more than a little coaxing to finally get her on the stand to tell the truth.

Prostitutes and Policing

In law enforcement, as in many other professions, young officers often follow in the footsteps of their mentors or, in our case, Field Training Officers (FTOs). If your FTO likes working DWIs you become an expert in breathalyzers and sobriety tests; if your FTO likes finding stolen cars, you become an expert in running plates and knowing where the hijacked vehicles are stripped and dumped.

For me, I was destined to work with prostitutes. Two of my three FTOs were famous for knowing the women of the street and for keeping peace on Dallas' most infamous prostitute stroll, Harry Hines Boulevard.

After my field training was complete, I was assigned to the heart of Harry Hines, and working the prostitutes became a nightly affair. Before long I had created my own "Hook Book" of regular prostitutes, pimps and "johns," and even older officers and investigators from downtown would ask for my help in tracking down one of the Harry Hines regulars.

Little did I know in the earliest days of my crime fighting career that the lessons I would learn would pave the way for my later days in Oak Cliff managing an unruly group of prostitutes and eventually shape the rest of my professional career.

Fortunately, most people never have to have any interactions with the drug-addled prostitutes that roam the streets in search of their next trick or easy victim of theft, so for the next little bit allow me to share with you a few words on the world's oldest profession.

If it Looks Like a Duck

Even after we had been dating a while, Jill still did not quite believe all of the stories she had heard about my exploits or antics as a police officer, until one night we attended a party where many of her family members were present. She proudly announced that I was a long-time Dallas police officer and that, although I was now stationed in Oak Cliff, the first portion of my career was spent working on Harry Hines Boulevard, a stretch of roadway in north Dallas not far from Love Field airport.

Harry Hines Boulevard is a major artery in that part of the city and is located adjacent to the IH-35 business corridor with the World Trade Center and major hotels, but the Hines strip itself had fallen into disrepair decades before. During my tenure in the Northwest Patrol Division, the area featured littered parking lots, rundown night clubs, and a host of topless and fully-nude bars.

Although some legitimate businesses thrived along Harry Hines, including the RV business where my wife's aunt and uncle worked, the area was better known for its seedy underbelly. It was one of the prime locations in Dallas for finding prostitutes. Not long after Jill's uncle and I were introduced, our conversation turned to exactly that topic.

Harry Hines has traditionally been a place where out-of-town businessmen and sports figures quenched both their thirst and their sexual appetites as they mixed and mingled with ladies of the evening. Hines was also well-known among local residents, and on more than one occasion professional athletes were caught using the services of women who were more than glad to take their money in exchange for a few minutes of fun.

Most of the women along Harry Hines were just street prostitutes working for local pimps, with a smattering of ladies employed by larger networks which occasionally sent them around the country to various high-profile events as a reward for doing well. Often the girls who worked for these prostitution rings would come back from Spring Training or preseason training with a host of stories and autographs from the men they entertained. Finally, a very small percentage of the women were working girls who had previously worked for escort services that placed women in some of the major hotels. They were girls who had fallen out of grace with their employers or who had lost their looks and had been reassigned to the streets, where their clientele really didn't care what they looked like as long as they performed what was asked of them.

My wife's uncle remembered those days when prostitutes could be found on nearly every corner along Hines, walking the side streets at all times of day looking to "flatback," or turn a quick trick to make their night's quota. But what amazed Jill was that he knew who I was, not so much by name but by reputation.

In minutes the stories were flying. He assured my wife that everything she had heard about me was probably more true than not. He also confirmed that although my ways might not have been conventional, within a few short years the working girls had been pushed to the back streets and the overall numbers significantly reduced.

I remember arresting so many prostitutes that the unfortunate officers who drove the paddy wagon would go to different parts of the city just so they didn't have to continually process all of the prostitutes that we arrested for Manifestation of Prostitution. That creative City charge essentially said that if you had a previous conviction for prostitution and were caught flagging down cars to attract potential customers, you could be arrested. On the street we called it the "duck law," assuming that if you looked like a duck and quacked like a duck, you were a duck.

We arrested lots of ducks.

In a business where time is money and time off the street is lost income, the girls (and more important, their pimps) soon learned that they had to find other places to ply their trade or lose serious revenue. Time in jail meant fines that had to be paid and lost income on the street. My then-partner (and still my best friend today) Brian Rippenkroeger and I made hundreds of arrests a year, and with a little creativity and some aggressive police work made a small difference in our little section of the city.

Little did I know then that the lessons I learned on the streets and about the prostitutes would set the tone for my entire career and beyond. I have more stories about prostitutes than anyone should have, because they have been my primary focus throughout my career. As a matter of fact, they played such an integral role in my solving Dallas' only serial killer case that one might say prostitutes made my career and pushed me into the national spotlight. Books, documentaries, and popular television shows have been adapted from my award-winning book *The Eyeball Killer*, and featured some of my exploits with the ladies of the night.

Jill (at that time my fiancé) used to tease me when we would be making our way from her family's north Oak Cliff home to some other destination in the city, and we'd pull up to a traffic light where the girls were working. They would wave and say "Hi, JJ!" — the name they knew me by from the street.

She would roll her eyes and ask, "How do you think it looks with us riding together, and all the working girls in this part of the city call you by name?"

But as an officer herself, she knew my reputation — or had at least heard stories — so she was never that bothered by the whole scene of crackheads waving "Hi' and offering to join me and my "friend" (for a reasonable fee, of course). She usually just laughed it off, especially when she learned my secret: when Dallas Police officers are in uniform, our name badge displays our first two initials followed by our last name. When working the streets, I would never tell any suspects or criminals my name, so they all referred to me as JJ. My friends and family knew that I detested nicknames and wanted to be called John, so if anytime I was in public and out of uniform and someone referred to me as JJ, I knew it wasn't a friend but rather someone from the street and, most likely, a criminal whom I had arrested.

J.J.

After working the streets for years, it still amazes me how many people from my past keep popping up, most of the time in the wrong place. Once I responded to a call at a well-known prostitute hotel; when I went busting in the door I was greeted by two familiar faces who both called out "Hi, JJ!" One of them was a well-known prostitute whom I had arrested scores of times; the other was a convicted murderer who I remembered arresting not long before. I drew down on him, thinking he was an escaped prisoner, until he produced a piece of paper stating that he had served all his time on the murder charge and was free and clear. I was stunned and called the jail for confirmation, but it was true. I had testified in his involuntary manslaughter case just over two years before, and because of the backlog in the criminal justice system and a ridiculously liberal application of 'good behavior' and 'time served' credit, he did his entire sentence in the county jail and never set foot in a prison.

So being called "JJ" by people on the street was nothing new. Officers usually deal with the same offenders over and over again as they move through the revolving doors of our criminal justice system.

It's when I am out shopping or with my family that hearing the familiar "JJ" gives me cause to pause.

On one occasion, I was in a Wal-Mart store 30 miles from the city and handed the gun counter attendant my driver's license in order to purchase a hunting license for the upcoming season. The man behind the counter entered all of the information, confirming my current address and phone number, and then looked at me and asked, "You don't remember me, do you, JJ?"

I'm sure my heart skipped a few beats, as I muttered, "No, I don't think so." I hoped he had entered all of my vital information into the state computer system without really paying attention to where I lived.

"You arrested me about eight years ago for felony drugs," he said, without looking up from the computer.

"I did?" I asked innocently, while running a number of really bad scenarios through my head. He was behind the gun counter with access to a virtual army's worth of guns and ammunition, holding my driver's license in my hand; I'm standing at the counter in my street clothes with my sidearm locked securely in my car out in the parking lot.

"This is not good," I thought to myself, as I strained to see if he had a gun within reach, and tried to figure out where I could jump in order to get out of his line of fire.

As my mind churned, the man turned his pock-marked face to me and smiled.

"I just want to thank you," he said. "You turned my life around. I went to jail, got into a program, and got straight, and I've been that way ever since." He held out his hand for me to shake.

"I'm glad I was able to help," I said. "Not a lot of people can pull that off and stay clean. You should give yourself credit because you deserve it," I said, while still looking for cover from gunfire if this conversation should take a turn for the worst. But he finished my transaction and I was on my way.

As I remember it, I almost ran from the store, hoping he would soon forget our conversation. And, most important, forget where I lived.

On another day I was out with my family at Chuck E. Cheese, a popular children's pizza restaurant, celebrating the birthday of one of my children's friends, when from somewhere behind the bouncy ball pit I heard "JJ, is that you? Hi, JJ!"

I looked over, thinking I couldn't be the one who was the target of the "JJ'ing," to see a rather large woman waving at me and hollering, "Oh, JJ!" I thought, My God, I can't even take the kids out without hearing my initials and wondering if they were going to be followed by cursing or a gun blast.

I told the kids we had to go, and apologized to our friends, knowing they would understand once we explained later. My wife wouldn't have wanted to leave, but she had heard the 'JJ' for herself, and she gathered up the kids. They would never have realized that the woman hollering at me was a former prostitute whom I had arrested on a dozen occasions, because in this setting she appeared as regular as the next person.

But that is one thing that officers who worked in Oak Cliff usually learned very quickly. In that fair section of the city, prostitutes don't wear furs, work out of high-dollar hotels, or dress like the "working girls" you see in the movies. On the streets of the inner city, there are no "pretty women" as portrayed by Julia Roberts in her popular movie role. These women are drug addicts and crack whores who work for a pimp and turn tricks to get high.

"Pretty Woman"

It never ceases to amaze me how the media, especially the motion picture industry, can glamorize individuals or groups of people who are far from glamorous. We have seen this time and time again, most often with criminals. From Billy the Kid to Bonnie and Clyde, Hollywood has made heroes out of outlaws.

For some reason they find selling these movies much easier, probably because the public "buys" the story, both literally and figuratively. It seems that even the most interesting of characters are not embraced by the movie moguls until they are spiced up a little bit. There always has to be more sex or more violence to add to the drama and make the plot more interesting, even if not plausible.

I wish those movie and TV producers would spend just a few minutes on my beat. Seeing what real prostitutes look like and how they live is anything but pretty. Give me just a few moments with them and I would introduce them to "pretty" women like Susan.

Her teeth (the ones she had left) were broken and stained, and her body odor was masked only by the repulsive breath she exhaled into the night air. The black straight hair was matted against her head. She wore the same clothes which had adorned her drug-emaciated figure for the past three days, and there was little prospect of her changing the filthy rags anytime soon. Tired and hungry, she had last slept about two and a half days ago, and she could not recall her last full meal.

Her bikini top left little to the imagination. She showed the world most of what she had been graced with, but in doing so she also revealed the scars left from a gunshot wound she suffered when a trick decided he would rather shoot her then pay her. Her bare arms revealed scars from multiple burns, grotesque souvenirs furnished by a former pimp as a reminder to her and other working girls of the price to be paid for not turning in their money at the end of the night.

Even a cursory visual examination revealed over a dozen prominent scars, and countless other abrasions and lacerations from nearly every type of imaginable and unthinkable encounter. She was a woman of the world, a woman of the streets. She was a prostitute, hooker, a lady of the evening. To the other prostitutes on the corner, she was just another "working girl."

Doesn't sound like those buxom beauties on television that portray the women who sell their bodies to the highest bidder, does it? That is because this is not television. This is the real world on the streets of Dallas. I am afraid that real life is just not as neat and pretty as those Hollywood movie sets.

In the real world, most of the street walkers are drug-crazed prostitutes who will do anything to get or stay high. Their life is far from elegant or glamorous. As a matter of fact, I would call it more of an existence than a life. They get by, day after day, by turning one trick and then another until they get enough money to go to the nearest drug den for another "hit" of dope.

Between the pimps, the police, the drug dealers and the perverted tricks, life on the streets is anything but a romantic Hollywood movie. In real life, the prostitutes simply try to stay out of jail and to stay high. They usually fail at both. The cycle of drugs is endless. If narcotics don't kill them, a trick probably will. If they are lucky, they will be arrested, where they can look forward to three square meals a day and a bed with clean sheets, both nearly impossible to find on the streets.

So the next time you are watching one of those glamorous cops & robbers shows, remember it is just a movie. Even though the characters may seem real, I can almost guarantee the real person probably wasn't a pretty woman.

Smiley

During my time behind the badge in Oak Cliff I came to know scores of these ladies of the evening, speed freaks, crack whores, and victims of abuse and violence, who all have their own stories of why they do what they do. Many of the girls I worked with on an almost-daily basis lived or worked around the Jefferson Boulevard/R.L.Thornton/Twelfth Street area of Oak Cliff, soliciting tricks from those who lived in, worked in, or just passed through this busy part of the community.

Just down the street was the house of a well-known pimp who had been running girls for as long as anyone could remember. Smiley was a unique individual who earned his nickname by always smiling and waving to the cops as they passed by. I'm sure he was thinking, "There's nothing you can do and we both know it, so have a good day." Smiley obviously had friends in high places; I always found it strange that everyone knew what was going on in and around that house, yet not a single case was ever made against him.

As a matter of fact, it seemed that every time we tried to apply pressure to his operation, some "important" crime matter would divert our resources.

It infuriated me that someone downtown was protecting Smiley from a host of "promoting prostitution" charges, but what would really infuriate me was the realization that for years he got away with torture, and probably more than a few murders. When girls would short him on money, he would handcuff them over a steel bar suspended from the ceiling, strip them, and then invite assorted friends to sexually assault and abuse them for hours and even days on end, during which time the perpetrators would burn them with cigarettes and cigars to permanently scar them, a visible reminder to both that girl and to other prostitutes that one does not steal from the boss.

Another popular form of punishment that Smiley meted out was breaking a girl's jaw, for not satisfying a well-paying customer who demanded certain sexual pleasures, or from talking back to the boss—or, for that matter, talking back to any one of his thug minions who often followed the girls from a distance, keeping an eye on the merchandise and counting the number of tricks turned so as to ensure that everyone got their share of the money. Once the punishment was administered (usually along with other forms of physical pain or torture), Smiley would have the offending girl taken to a doctor or quasi-medical professional with whom he had a relationship, and order that the girl's jaw be wired open just far enough so that she could continue to work. A girl who was not making money was of no use to him. Once repaired, the girl would immediately be dispatched back to the streets so that she could pay off the medical bills Smiley had incurred on her behalf.

As conscientious police officers and just concerned citizens, we would try to warn prostitutes their lifestyles were deadly, but few listened. I would tell them there are usually only two end results in their line of work—prison or death—but few would heed the warnings.

I would see these working women on a daily basis, hear their life stories on the way to jail, and see their addictions in the track marks on their arms, legs, and between their toes. I felt strange when my own prophecies became reality and I read the name of one of these street walkers in a homicide report, or was summoned to the Medical Examiner's office to identify yet another body.

Raz

How can I forget the day I walked into the station and was immediately summoned to respond to a crime scene where one of the ladies of the evening had been found dead in a drainage ditch? The detectives at the scene needed a little help from a street officer, because apparently her assailant had cut off her head and taken it with him.

I hurried out to the location and before I even crawled into the drainage ditch I yelled to the Homicide investigators, "Yep, that's Raz all right; her real name is Rachael."

"Are you sure?" they asked as I made my way down next to the naked body.

"No doubt about it," I said, "Raz is the only tall, thin and decent looking girl brunette on this end of the strip—and besides, I would recognize that tattoo on her left shoulder anywhere.

"I've arrested her dozens of times over the past few years and listed the tattoo on her arrest reports. I even have it noted right here in my Hook Book," I said, pointing to the small notebook I kept in my uniform pocket with pictures and detailed descriptions of the working girls and their activities. Nearly every officer who worked during that time had their own version of a hook book, but depending on what area of the city you worked and the majority of the offenses you responded to, one might have lists of burglars, while another listed robbers and rapists.

"Any reason you know of someone might want her dead?" the investigators continued their questioning of me as I examined the body.

"She's a street whore; there are a million reasons to kill a hooker: don't want anyone to know what you did so you eliminate the witness; didn't get the services you paid for; got ripped off earlier and came back to get revenge; but I say this is not the work of your average trick. My money is on the pimp for this one. Trying to send a message to the other girls, I'm guessing," I continued in my best detective voice.

I could tell they were getting annoyed by me because of course I was just a street cop—but remember *they* called *me* and asked for my help.

"Any guess on who did this, Dick Tracy?" one of the detectives indignantly asked.

"Of, course" I responded, "I probably even know where you can find the head," I said as I walked away from the homicide professionals out of the culvert and toward my squad car. My body language must have spoken volumes, and clearly signaled that my assistance had come to a screeching halt.

"OK, I'm sorry," I heard the older investigator who had made the Dick Tracy comment.

"I said, I'm sorry for the comment, do you know who her pimp is?" the detective asked.

I had my back to them now and was already looking up the name and address.

"His name is Jamal and you can find him at this address in West Dallas," I said to the detectives as I tossed them a piece of paper from my Hook Book with all of the information they needed.

"As a matter of fact," I continued without any prompting, "my guess is you will find Raz's head somewhere close by, because why would he take it unless he was trying to make a bold statement to the other girls?" I surmised.

Without even a "thank you" from my new-found friends, I returned to my squad car and began my shift on the street. But first I took out a black marker and wrote across the page of information in my Hook Book describing Raz and her activities: **DECEASED**. She now joined scores of other pages with the same label.

And, by the way, the next day I learned from some other whores that the investigators did go to the pimp's house and found Raz's head, and arrested him for murder. It was an easy case to make as Jamal had killed Raz in the ditch, cut off her head and driven it around the city, showing it to all of his working girls before placing it in the room where most of them slept in his West Dallas house. Case closed, another murder solved, and like so many others I'm still waiting on that "thank you" from Homicide for doing their work.

Arresting a Serial Killer

The briefing is held at Central Patrol Division, home to the Dallas Police Department's Tactical Team. Inside the primary roll call room, no words are uttered, but anyone within earshot can hear the unmistakable sounds of a small army of SWAT officers donning their life-saving gear. Highly trained peacekeepers pull specially designed Kevlar vests with embedded steel chest plates over their shoulders, and strap the entire assembly tightly around their bodies. The vests must be properly positioned and secured so that all vital organs are protected during a fistfight or firefight, but still allow enough room for officers to breathe during a stressful tactical entry or physical encounter with a suspect.

Boots strapped on tightly—no loose laces to trip on during the operation—and Sam Browne-style nylon belts with their variety of tactical accoutrements: semi-automatic handgun, Taser, handcuffs, flexi cuffs, retractable baton and pepper spray, are clicked into position. Every item is precisely placed on each individual's belt to maximize muscle memory and minimize thinking: there's no time to think when one's life is on the line.

I reach for my own sidearm as I've done a thousand times over the years, to reassure myself of the exact position of my Sig Saur P226 9mm semi-automatic pistol. Checking and rechecking, I feel the two additional magazines on my left side; counting the one in my gun with a round already chambered, that makes a total of 46 bullets at my immediate disposal if the night turns really ugly. I look up to see other officers going through the same routine, checking their side arms, tactical assault rifles, night scopes, night vision goggles, and even stun grenades. Weapons, ammunition, and equipment are all checked and rechecked in the noisy silence, until the Tactical Commander starts the briefing with his straightforward baritone command of "Listen up."

The room turns quiet as one of the FBI agents who had been staking out an Oak Cliff residence for the past several hours approaches the chalkboard, which bears a crude drawing of a simple wood framed house and detached garage. During their surveillance, agents have determined that there is a closed-in front porch which leads into the main living area, the kitchen is in the rear of the house with a back door off of a utility area, and the bedrooms and bathroom appear to be on the right side of the residence.

Additional information could be obtained if there were more time, but there is no more time: with each tick of the clock, another woman could be disappearing into the darkness of Dallas.

Officers like me who have worked in "The Cliff," the local colloquial term for the section of Dallas known as Oak Cliff, are familiar with the area around the suspected killer's house. For years many of us have given "tours" for visiting dignitaries, officers from other jurisdictions, and Kennedy assassination enthusiasts. Ironically, the suspected killer's house is located right around the corner from the former residence of Lee Harvey

Oswald, accused assassin of President John F. Kennedy. Somehow this seems a fitting location for Dallas's latest publicity nightmare: a serial killer who prowls the streets nightly in search of women he can abuse, torture, and kill, and whose eyes he removes before leaving their naked or partially clad bodies on display in the street for all to see.

The briefing continues with specific plans for the assault on the house, along with individual assignments for all officers. The battering ram will be used to bust in the front door, hopefully dislodging any locks or security devices and providing an opening for the stun grenades, serving as the 'shock and awe' portion of the assault prior to the insertion of the Entry Team. If the surprise attack in the middle of the night is successful, the suspected killer will be quickly taken into custody by the Arrest Team.

If there is no resistance, the entire operation should take only seconds to accomplish.

With the plan now in place, the briefing is concluded with the baritone orders of "Load up!" Instantly the room springs to life as officers grab their gear and hustle into waiting vehicles. It's after midnight and some of us have been working since seven in the morning, but not a tired or bleary eye can be found. Too much adrenaline, too much at stake, too many dead girls.

As the vehicles are loaded, everyone knows it all ends tonight, one way or another.

The suspected killer is a sociopath, a convicted felon, most likely armed with multiple weapons and believed to be well practiced in the art of killing. He will most likely face the death penalty, so he has nothing to lose by taking out as many officers as possible. He might even be planning an ambush, guaranteeing additional media coverage and morning headlines that will no doubt add to his criminal resume and deadly legacy.

To minimize any potential loss of life, everyone agrees the assault must be a total surprise. No lights or sirens, no tactical vehicles, just nondescript unmarked passenger vans with dark tinted windows.

As soon as the signal is given, the caravan with its heavily armed cadre of local officers and federal agents winds its way through the maze of downtown streets, across the Jefferson viaduct, and into north Oak Cliff. Federal agents who have been staking out the house for hours believe the suspect is inside, but cannot confirm it because a priority call forced them to abandon the stakeout for a brief period of time, just long enough for an elusive killer to slip through their hands.

But the decision has already been made, the judge awakened from his sleep to sign a warrant, and the tactical team called in to use their special skills and equipment. It is now or never.

It begins. The door goes crashing inward, sending all of the locks and most of the doorframe flying across the small living room. Not one, but two explosions immediately follow as the flash-and-bang devices ignite, lighting up the entire front portion of the house and setting the living room couch on fire. Without the slightest hesitation, the Entry Team fights through the broken door amidst smoke, fire, screams, and cries. The suspected killer is literally blown out of his bed and into the arms of Entry Team officers, who secure him and hand him off to the awaiting Arrest Team.

It all occurs in the blink of an eye.

My heart is pounding, nearly beating out of my chest. This is the biggest arrest of my career, the case of a lifetime that will be placed squarely at my feet, since I am the officer who solved the case and convinced DPD Homicide, the FBI, and the Dallas County District Attorney's Office of the identity of the killer. Sweat beads on my forehead and drips onto my uniform as the Arrest Team motions for me to come forward.

I move into the living room as two officers lift the prisoner to his feet. Nearby, a false fireplace hides a cache of weapons and physical evidence linking the killer to his latest victim. The Sergeant motions towards the prisoner's wrist, a signal to me to handcuff the confined man. It is a sign of respect for my contribution to the arrest. Quickly the links of my Smith & Wesson handcuffs clink into place and I turn to escort the serial killer to my squad car, and to eventual justice.

I didn't know it at the time, but this arrest would change my life forever: the arrest of Dallas's only serial killer, book and movie deals, television shows, and media appearances that would lead to a 30-year career in law enforcement and private consulting.

But on that night as I escorted my prisoner out of his smoke-filled house of horrors, my bullet-proof vest and its steel chest plate could barely contain my pounding heart. After nearly 24 hours without sleep, months of investigation, and too many dead women, I couldn't believe it was finally over.

As I turned my squad car around in the street and headed towards homicide with my prize catch, I thought to myself, "This is going to make a great column."

About the Author

John Matthews is the Executive Director of the Community Safety Institute (CSI) and also serves as an Assistant Chief Deputy Constable for Dallas County Precinct #1. Matthews has been in law enforcement for more than 30 years, and is a Master Peace Officer and certified law enforcement instructor. With Bachelor's and Master's degrees in Administrative Management and an Advanced Law Enforcement Certificate, Matthews is nationally recognized for his work in law enforcement and school safety issues, and has been honored as a keynote speaker at law enforcement conferences around the country.

John is an award-winning writer and the author of seven books including *The Eyeball Killer*, a true crime Book of the Month and firsthand account of his capture of Dallas' only serial killer. In *Mass Shootings: Six Steps to Survival*, he examines four decades of these deadly crimes and presents an easy-to-remember model for survival. His books *School Safety 101*, *Creating a Safer School*, and *Neighborhood Watch 101* focus on making our communities safer and more secure, and have been the cornerstones of training programs for thousands of law enforcement officers, educators, and community stakeholders.

John currently serves as a law enforcement analyst for both CNN and FOX News, where he has made multiple appearances providing analysis on breaking public safety stories. For three years he was a talk show host on KRLD/CBS radio and the Texas State Network and hosted a safety segment on FOX-4 television. Media appearances include the *Sean Hannity Show*, CNN, ABC, CBS and *NBC News*, *FOX News Channel*, *Leeza*, *The O'Reilly Report*, *Good Morning New York*, *Good Morning Texas*, *Law Enforcement Television Network*, *A Current Affair*, *Good Day Dallas*, *Discovery Channel*, and scores of local ABC, CBS, FOX and NBC television and radio affiliates. His serial killer story has been featured on shows including HBO Autopsy, Evil I, and Very Bad Men, and been adapted for network television shows.

As a Texas lawman, entrepreneur and writer, John garnered a host of awards. He was named *Outstanding Law Enforcement Officer* and awarded a Certificate of Commendation from the Texas State Senate. He received numerous awards from the Dallas Police Department including *Certificate of Merit, Life Saving Award, Certificate for Civic Achievement,* and the *Police Commendation.* He has been honored with the ACE National Education Award, and both the Texas and International Downtown Association awards for building public/private partnerships. He has received three ACE National Entrepreneurship awards, an INC. 500 award, a Venture 100 award, and a Texas Press Association award for column writing.

John has served as a Senior Advisor to the National Sheriffs' Association, and currently is the Director of Federal Partnerships for the National Law Enforcement Officers Memorial Fund.

Community Safety Institute has developed more than 100 law enforcement and public safety initiatives for the federal government including the *Creating a Safer School* (CASS) for school districts; the *National Neighborhood Watch Training Program* and *Toolkit*; the *Continuity of Operations Planning for Sheriffs*; the Destination Zero program and the National Officer Safety and Wellness Awards; the *Public Safety De-escalation Tactics for Military Veterans in Crisis* (PSDTMVC) and the *PSDTMVC Trainer-of Trainers* for the Bureau of Justice Assistance (BJA); the *Safe School* program and *Juvenile Justice* series for the Office of Juvenile Justice and Delinquency Prevention (OJJDP); *Law Enforcement and Mental Health Partnerships*, the *STAR Initiative*, *Native American Training Series I, II, III* and *IV; the Contracting for Public Safety Services Model, the Cross-Deputation in Indian Country* project, *the Animal Cruelty as a Gateway to More Serious Crimes* project, *Human Trafficking in Indian Country, Creating Collaborative Partnerships Between Casino Security and Tribal Police,* and the *Jail Information Model* for the Office of Community Oriented Policing Services (COPS); the *Basic Law Enforcement Supervisory Training Program* and the *Command Officer Leadership Series* for the Department of the Interior, Office of Justice Services (OJS); the Readiness and Emergency Management School Safety Program for the Department of Education grantees; the online Village Public Safety Officer (VPSO) training program, Alaska State Troopers and Alaska Wildlife Troopers courses for the Alaska Department of Public Safety; the Officer Safety Initiatives for the DOT National Highway Traffic Safety Administration (NHTSA); multiple Weapons of Mass Destruction programs for the Department of Homeland Security (DHS); and online training courses for the National Crime Prevention Council.

Made in the USA
Monee, IL
31 May 2023

34317751R00129